"This book is a bright lant
of your mind and heart, (
tice, and love. Ralph utilizes personal stories of radical healing combined with wisdom from meditation, neuroscience, psychotherapy, activism, and music to make complex theory accessible and relevant. A stunning and transformative book, critical for our times."

» YAEL SHY
author of *What Now? Meditation for Your Twenties and Beyond*

"Stepping onto the path of radical self-inquiry just got a little easier with Ralph De La Rosa's guidance. With his requisite punk-rock sensibilities, deep spiritual practice, and years of clinical practice, Ralph goes beyond the usual platitudes and teaches us all how to navigate those times when we're *not* so mindful, when we've become entangled in a web spun of anger, fear, and shame. Ralph's wit, wisdom, and practical advice were the antidotes I needed in these anxious times to exhale completely and recommit to a life of service."

» LINDA SPARROWE
author of *Yoga at Home* and *Yoga Mama*

"This book is like a flotation device amid the churning waters of insanity—not only in the world we live in but inside our bodies and minds as well."

» WILL JOHNSON
author of *The Posture of Meditation* and *Breathing as Spiritual Practice*

"Through his experience as a psychotherapist, author, storyteller, and meditation teacher, Ralph De La Rosa sheds light upon the crucial subject of emotional resilience. He masterfully blends science with love to help us understand that we are all able to mention, and manage, our emotions through self-healing, mindfulness, and growth."

» BRENDAN BURNS
host of *The Brendan Burns Show*

For anyone lost in the dense forest
*   of the world without a compass.*

For anyone left in the dark without
*   a match to make fire.*

For anyone caught in cycles
*   of systemic confusion and cruelty.*

For anyone who has known bedtime
*   without dinner. Or breakfast.*

For anyone who has never felt listened to.
*   Or loved.*

For anyone so stressed or scared that they've
*   forgotten to savor the sky and the rain.*

For every wolf that roams.

DON'T
TELL ME TO
RELAX

Emotional Resilience
in the Age of Rage, Feels,
and Freak-Outs

RALPH DE LA ROSA

SHAMBHALA

Shambhala Publications, Inc.
4720 Walnut Street
Boulder, Colorado 80301
www.shambhala.com

Cover design: Daniel Urban-Brown
Interior design: Kate Huber-Parker

9 8 7 6 5 4 3 2 1

First Edition
Printed in the United States of America

⊗ This edition is printed on acid-free paper that meets the
American National Standards Institute Z39.48 Standard.
♻ This book is printed on 30% postconsumer recycled paper.
For more information please visit www.shambhala.com.
Shambhala Publications is distributed worldwide by
Penguin Random House, Inc., and its subsidiaries.

Library of Congress Cataloging-in-Publication Data
Names: De La Rosa, Ralph, author.
Title: Don't tell me to relax: emotional resilience
in the age of rage, feels, and freak-outs / Ralph De La Rosa.
Other titles: Do not tell me to relax
Description: First Edition. | Boulder: Shambhala, 2020.
Identifiers: LCCN 2019053705 | ISBN 9781611808407 (trade paperback)
Subjects: LCSH: Self-control. | Emotions. | Self-actualization (Psychology)
Classification: LCC BF632 .D425 2020 | DDC 158.1—dc23
LC record available at https://lccn.loc.gov/2019053705

Para mi madre.

∧ ∧ ∧

When the chips were down,
you came through for us.
Like a lioness.

It's chaos.
Be kind.

—*Michelle McNamara*

CONTENTS

DON'T
TELL
ME
TO
RELAX

INTRODUCTION
Waking Up in a World on Fire

If you are falling . . . *dive.*
—*Joseph Campbell*

Samsara davanala nada lida lokah. "Being caught up in this world is like sleeping in a forest fire." These were the first words from my lips each morning during my brief foray into Vedic monasticism. Fresh out of a cold shower at 4 a.m., we'd gather in the temple room to sing the *mangal aarthi* (or "most auspicious ceremony" in Sanskrit). It's striking that this celebratory, devotional ritual opens with such a grim admission—that the forest fires of crisis (be they personal or global) are not only inherent in this life but that they become so normalized that *we can fall asleep in them.* Yet, it's only a matter of time before a burning ember lands on our pillow.

The *mangal aarthi* is far from a manifesto of cynicism, though. This particular stanza is intended to incite a liberating sense of urgency. It connotes, "Seeing this, we must refuse to rest on our laurels. We must rise. We must find the path home. We must make sure no one is left behind. We cannot put this off until tomorrow." It's a call to confront the status quo of our lives. A needed kick in the arse for a somnambulistic human race. It points us toward a secret truth known to the ancient yogis and meditators—that the trouble and disaster inherent in this life can become an endless wellspring of inspiration when we know how to meet it. The old-schoolers knew about a door to freedom that opens when we turn toward our distress and its sources rather than away from them. They also knew that this was not a religious or sectarian truth but a universal one that belongs to us all.

The devotional hymn, or *kirtan*, goes on to speak of an "ocean of mercy" that is capable of extinguishing the heat of the suffering world. It tells us that such a boon could only be delivered through the strength of intelligent self-inquiry combined with courageous, compassionate action. The ocean of mercy is formed by our willingness to embody a better way—a deeper way, a daringly heartfelt way, a humane way both fierce and tender in its approach. It is then made manifest when we stand for and enact that very way in the world. The verse, then, frames meditation and wakeful living *not* as a set of personal stress-reduction techniques but as a systemic approach to life, one that is capable of informing our responses to the most calamitous of situations. The verse frames meditation as a form of disaster preparedness.

The disaster, my friends, is here.

⌃ ⌃ ⌃

"Like sleeping in a forest fire." I appreciate the disruptive honesty of this phrase now more than ever. Our world is burning, being ravaged by the gross misuse of power right before our eyes. At the time of this writing, three-quarters of the way into 2019, we've had more mass shootings than days of the year in the United States.[1] Record-breaking climate disasters abound with increasing frequency amid the dismantling of the Environmental Protection Agency. Approximately fifteen thousand undocumented immigrant children sit in overcrowded cages—alone, traumatized, separated from their loved ones—in some two hundred for-profit detention centers in unsanitary and unlivable conditions. White nationalists in openly racist organizations have not only come out of the closet, they're being retweeted and referred to as "very fine people" by the president of the United States. Working poor and middle-class families continue to struggle mightily while violence, police brutality, and drug addiction soar in impoverished, disproportionately black and Latinx communities.

The bubbles have burst and the masks have come off. Shaken from our slumber, we must now figure out how to address an unprecedentedly distressing situation. Our limbic systems are pumping cortisol and adrenaline into our bodies with every disaster we read about, with every dangerous reality we face. The constant stream of algorithmically curated clickbait headlines can make it tough to tune out the noise and focus on the actual injustice around the world and even—maybe especially—in our own backyards.

Staring down the barrel of a global crisis, we might assume that things like emotional intelligence, neuropsychological insight, and meditation are beside the point. It might seem that we ought to be laser-focused on concrete solutions and actions. Those who doubt the efficacy of more inwardly focused practices to support social change aren't misguided. The capitalist appropriation of meditation and wellness culture isn't just disheartening; it too often places such inner technology out of the reach of those who need it most. What was designed as a means for getting all sentient beings out of the fires has, in many spheres, been reduced to a strategy for the optimization of privilege. Meditation can and has been co-opted by our overarching tendency to numb and distract ourselves in the face of difficulty; it can and has been used to quell our sense of urgency about our current and impending global crises. That which could summon an ocean of mercy is being reduced to a sophisticated form of naptime.

Such trends cannot corrupt the integrity of the practice itself (and, while we're here, neither can any of the reprehensible scandals that have gone on with some of the more visible spiritual teachers in recent years). Meditation is a vehicle that can uncover indomitable compassion and an earnest desire to lift each other up. Nothing can change that, and there are thousands of spiritual communities and secular mindfulness spaces that promote the true spirit and intention of the practice. Yet, even in such groups, one often finds a prevailing belief among practitioners that spiritual practice and politics should have little to do with one another—a belief so strong that it has led many such communities to institute formal or informal taboos on discussing "political" topics in their practice spaces.

Such situations are what inspired the title of this book. I take "don't tell me to relax" as a mantra of empowerment. It connotes our willingness to confront that which is corrosive to our inherent dignity as beings and the survival, both literally and figuratively, of humanity. That said, this book could just as easily have been titled "Don't Tell Me How to Feel." The matter at hand isn't about whether or not we ought to relax—a question that is, after all, entirely contextual—but about our inherent right to have and express feelings about dehumanization. Others may urge us to channel our anger with "civility" or call us "unhinged" for being hurt, angry, or terrified at what we are faced with. To be told we ought to feel some other way is the epitome of adding insult to injury. It's a terrible irony to express anger about harm and atrocity only to have people take issue with our anger as opposed to the harm and atrocity. This book is about how we can wash the salt from such wounds.

If you're a young person who can't understand why the adults in your life don't seem all that concerned about the future of our planet; if you're a woman being mansplained and then told you're overreacting when you bristle; if you're a person of color walking into a hostile white space for the umpteenth time this week (or a white space where everyone acts precious about your presence because they're trying to #staywoke)—you have every reason to not calm down. If you're an older person whose heart is breaking over the loss of urban neighborhoods or wild spaces you've loved your whole life; if you're here, queer, and refuse to get used to the way you are treated; if you're someone suffering from mental health issues in a world where we are disbelieved or blamed for our symptomology at every turn; if you work your ass off every week and still can't afford health insurance, student loan bills, or childcare; if you carry none of those identities but know in your bones that business as usual in our society cannot go on, let us join arms as we sing in heavenly refrain, "Don't you *dare* tell us to relax." Our anger is moral. Our rage is sacred. Our anxiety contains wisdom. Our hearts are telling us the truth. If the truth makes others uncomfortable—good. Show me an alarm clock that makes a sweet sound and I'll show you an alarm clock I can sleep through.

And—there's a catch.

Working with traumatized children and families was over-whelming for me at first. Though I've always reminded my-self, "I'm not the one having the bad day here," the interface that my job entailed with mass-scale poverty, sexual abuse, and physical abuse, as well as the systemic abuse delivered by the family court system itself—it was enough to break anybody. In my earliest days working in clinical foster care,

I was constantly distressed, and it showed. A senior administrator stopped me in the hall one day and, unprompted, advised me, "Don't worry. You'll grow a thick skin soon. And then it'll get better." I pointed to the center of my chest, to my heart, and responded, "No, thanks. This thing is my compass. I'm dead in the water without it." Though still wrestling with the question of how to walk through it all, I knew the answer couldn't be to "grow a thick skin." Thick skin, after all, is a callous. And to become calloused in the process of compassionate action simply makes no sense.

When I did find the answer, it was actually the exact opposite of growing a thick skin. Things got better when I allowed myself to become even more tender, to be even more connected to my emotions and reactions than ever before—to let the anguish-ridden realities set before me to kick my ass, even. I needed to stop thinking I ought to feel some other way and allow myself to feel into the truth of what I was presented with. That was step one. And this opened the door to step two. With my resistance to so-called negative feelings set aside, I could then tend to the hurting and distressed parts of myself with compassion and help those parts heal. In this way, I could feel what was natural for me to feel and let it give rise to self-compassion in me (which then increased my capacity for compassion for others). These two steps formed a sustainable way through the forest, a resilient way that not only was callous-free but also sparked unexpected growth in my life. This kind of self-compassion is a big part of what this book is about. Sure, it can look like taking breaks, celebrating life, and engaging in self-care to take the edge off—things I hope we all know to do by now. But I will argue that we need deeper medicine than that, too. Beyond emotional triage and self-maintenance, we need processes that alchemize our emotions and natural reactions: processes that uncover the transformative potency latent in our reactions and lead to lasting shifts in our lives (and thus in the actions that we take).

Repressing and contorting our emotions is unsustainable and unnatural. And yet, in the exact same breath that we own our anxiety, concern, and rage, we must also acknowledge that these feelings will harden us if we don't develop compassionate skills of emotional resilience. We cannot afford to stay flooded with toxic cortisol and adrenaline if we intend to stay in the ring long-term. (Please stay.) We cannot confront cruelty effectively if we lose touch with our hearts. We cannot lose sight of the larger view. We cannot afford to burn out. We need practices that will help us connect to our deeper wisdom in the face of crisis. We need ways to remember that the fight for justice is synonymous with a celebration of humanity. We need methods that help us to stay clear even as we stumble in the thick, gray fog. A path of "both/and" rather than "either/or." After all, embracing the interdependence of inner life and outer engagement was precisely the aim of many spiritual traditions at their outset.

᭢ ᭢ ᭢

Having a strong awareness and effective methodologies for working with one's own mind and heart has, if anything, become increasingly essential. To "resist psychic death," as the Bikini Kill song goes, is crucial. It's true that meditation and healing can be misappropriated as distancing mechanisms to quell the edge of anxiety we *ought* to feel about the despair of others. Such spiritual bypassing, is, in fact, a form of psychic death. I can assure you such is not this book's MO. We will instead be immersing ourselves in a worldview one finds in both Eastern and Western traditions: in Robert Frost's maxim that "the way out is through"; in the Tibetan principle that "the obstacle is the path"; in Gloria Steinem's reminder that "the truth will set you free, but first it'll piss you off." My friends, we are here to meet and wrestle with our situation. This is our mountain, and it must be moved.

How we move it matters. We can shout "Be the change" until we're blue in the face, and yet the question remains: "How?" How do we embody love, justice, decency, strong ethics, wisdom, and sanity when we're fighting to hold down a fire line? How, amid all this heat and smoke, do we remind ourselves to stay on a middle path between the extremes of paralyzing outrage and apathetic dissociation? Consider this book a field guide to finding your own answers to such questions, to locating your own inherent wisdom within the blaze.

⌃ ⌃ ⌃

Here's what I really want you to know:

> » **We need you.** Your presence here on this planet really matters. In each moment you are setting off a ripple effect that touches all beings either explicitly or implicitly. It's safe to say that you matter more than you or I can even fathom. What you do with your time and resources is of the utmost importance. And as Hallmark-card-cheesy as this sounds, you are a gift to the rest of us. It is a privilege to have you living and breathing in this world. I know that sometimes it feels like you're screaming at a tidal wave and making no difference. I know that sometimes you wish you could take a long, pizza-fueled nap and have the rest of us wake you when it's over. But we need you. We need the unique contribution you're here to make, now like never before. If you don't make the contribution you were born to make, it will be lost forever. Please do not keep it from us.

» **We need your emotions.** Emotions are the very center of our lives. Whether acknowledged or not, they drive everything we perceive, believe, think, say, and do. From one vantage point, your emotional state is the most important variable in any situation. It not only influences all your output; it filters everything you take in as well. Thing is—in case you haven't noticed—our emotions aren't up to us. What we do with them, however, is absolutely up to us. The parts of us that express our afflictive emotions are very much like people. If we relate to them with understanding and care, there tends to be one kind of outcome. If we relate to them by shoving them in the basement or forcing them to change, we get another kind of outcome.

Or maybe it's like this:

» Our emotions are like cats. You can ignore them all you want but eventually they will poop in your bed to get your attention.
» Our emotions are like dogs. You can throw shoes at them to get them to shut up but that only teaches them to attack you later.
» Our emotions are like liquor. They can intoxicate us, and we can stumble into addictive patterns with them.
» Our emotions are like children. Hold them firmly with love, just like you would a baby, and they will grow to be healthy. They will, over time, become a source of inner harmony, healing, and intuition. This book is about learning how to do just that.

» **We need a new paradigm of emotional resilience.** We've inherited an understanding and view in which emotions are erroneously considered irrational and in need of control. This model tells us our two choices are either to be consumed by our emotions or to push them away, to indulge them or repress them. It's a *static paradigm* that treats our emotional parts as if they're one-dimensional objects, as if they're not living, embodied forces inside of us that have inherent value and intelligence. This view not only plays an enormous role in perpetuating our pain, shame, and fear but also contributes greatly to the normalization of violence and exploitation in our societies.

Thankfully, the static paradigm is not our only option. A range of psychological modalities are offering new, emergent paradigms of emotional intelligence and resilience that are much more scientifically informed and lead us down more humane roads. At the leading edge of this paradigm shift is the radical psychological modality Internal Family Systems (IFS), which informs this book to a great degree.* IFS offers us a paradigm of allowing space for our vari-

---

* Internal Family Systems is an integrative psychotherapeutic approach first developed by Richard Schwartz. Drawing on systems thinking and family systems theory, Schwartz and others have created a model of relating to one's inner parts as discrete subpersonalities and tending to their various needs and concerns rather than ignoring or pathologizing them. Although, as will be clear, I draw tremendous inspiration from the IFS model in this book and share some of its terminology, I also use different language than is typically used in IFS, where inner parts are generally grouped as "managers," "firefighters," and "exiles." For readers interested in learning more about IFS, I highly recommend Schwartz's work. See, for instance, his audiobook, *Greater Than the Sum of Our Parts: Discovering Your True Self Through Internal Family Systems Therapy* (Louisville, CO: Sounds True, 2018).

ous emotions to be present so that we can learn how to be *with* our emotional parts as opposed to *in* them. From such a place, we can begin to uncover insights and useful information that they hold for us, reclaim the vital energy our emotions tend to eat up, and help to unburden the parts of us that have become stuck in patterns of wounding and defense. It's a *process paradigm* that treats our emotional parts as the dynamic, multidimensional, and intelligent energies that they are. It's an invitation to shift the kinds of conversations we're having within ourselves, which then shifts everything about how we show up in the outer world. Such a process paradigm is in direct alignment with approaches to emotional life present in Tibetan Buddhism (experiential *mahamudra* practices and some forms of *Vajrayana maitri* meditation present in the Kagyu and Nyingma lineages, specifically), and it's also taught by many renowned American *Theravadin* Buddhist teachers such as Tara Brach and Jack Kornfield. This is, in part, because the emotional process paradigm often opens the doorway to a direct experience of our deeper nature—an energy of self-compassion that allows "be the change" to start at home, in the human heart, where matters of justice begin and end.

» **We need to bring compassion and curiosity to our outrage and worry.** The static emotional paradigm has taught us our emotions are mutually exclusive. That is, if I'm feeling compassion, I'm not feeling anger; if I'm feeling devastated about the decimation of human life, I don't have room for joy or gratitude. Thankfully, this is false. Our synaptic networks have plenty of operating capacity for our so-called positive and so-called negative emotions to coexist. The truth is, we can marry compassion to our rage, we can use curiosity to clarify our anxiety, and we can mix empathy in with any gradient of emotional responsiveness. Practicing that in real time may sound complex and challenging, but I've been working with this kind of emotional alchemy long enough to know—it just takes practice and guidance. So, *hello.* This book is here to help.

» **We need to pendulate.** A pendulum swings back and forth, eventually traversing the entire area of a circle. This can serve as a model for our lives. In the evidence-based therapeutic modality Somatic Experiencing, one way that pendulation is practiced is by building psycho-emotional bridges between stronger parts of ourselves and those that are more wounded and reactive (such as bringing compassion to our rage, as described above). That's pendulation in the immediate sense, a way we can practice it on the spot. The concept of pendulation can apply to our lives and communities in a larger sense as well. There are times when we need to go all the way into the more challenging side of the spectrum (e.g., doing inner trauma work and healing, doing outer activist work, having tough conversations with people, asking ourselves the hard questions, making behavioral changes to bring our lives into alignment with our values); then there are times when we need to let all that go as much as possible and swing to the other side (e.g., basking in simple delights such as the warmth of the sun or the comfort of a song, practicing genuine self-love and deep self-care, releasing ourselves from perfectionism and worry, and savoring our messy and problematic lives just as they are). Like the Earth orbiting the sun, we, too, need to allow for and honor seasons in our lives. A time for things to bloom, a time for things to hibernate, a time for things to go through changes and uncertainty.

⌃ ⌃ ⌃

In my last book, *The Monkey Is the Messenger: Meditation and What Your Busy Mind Is Trying to Tell You,* I introduced the term *radical nonpathology.* Radical nonpathology is the antithesis to the medical model taken up by conventional psychology and even some proponents of Eastern spirituality. The medical model is rooted in the notion that if somebody has a symptom of some sort, there is a disease down below: *there is something wrong with the person that ought to be fixed.* A nonpathological model, then, is rooted in the notion that there isn't *anything* wrong with any of us. Nonpathology sees symptoms, even painful ones, as evidence of our innate drive toward health and well-being. A fever, for example, is just your body "cooking" a virus or bacteria out of you. The symptom of a fever isn't evidence of an inherent problem in your body. It's evidence of your body's innate intelligence, responsiveness, resilience, and robust drive toward health. Hence, radical nonpathology: the audacious notion that our wholeness as beings precedes all else. The splendor of our being (*ziji* in Tibetan) is what's primary, and the troubles in our lives are actually much more meaningful than we take them to be. The troubles in our lives are alarm bells that wake us up and incite our motivation to find a deeper way. They are, therefore, precious.

This book retains the focus on radical nonpathology, embedding it in an *empowerment model*: the truth that the inherent wisdom, clarity, and freedom of our deeper nature need not wait for anyone or anything else to come along. We can begin allowing our wiser nature to emerge now, right in the midst of the mess. We can begin taking ownership of our lives and actions regardless of what's coming at us. We must. We cannot afford to live in a perpetual mode of reactivity any longer. The "I do what I do because you did what you did"[*] model is about as third-grade as it gets. That's the burnout model, the static model, the grow-a-callous-over-your-heart-to-survive model. We can do better.

Our inherent power is the greatest resource we have. This was known to Frederick Douglass when he wrote, "I prayed for twenty years but received no answer until I prayed with my legs." It was known to James Baldwin when he wrote, "Freedom is not something that anybody can be given; freedom is something people take and people are as free as they want to be." It was known to Viktor Frankl when he penned, "Everything can be taken from a [person] but one thing: the last of the human freedoms—to choose one's attitude in any given set of circumstances, to choose one's own way." Such genuine empowerment seems to be accessed most deeply in counterintuitive ways—by communicating when we'd rather shut down, by becoming more aware when we'd rather sleep-walk, by choosing the vulnerability of connection when it would be easier to stay walled off, by digging deeper for new and more evolved ways, by caring.

Now, *there's* a word: caring. At a time when a prevailing maxim is to "give no fucks," a trope so tantalizing it has been turned into bestselling books, allow me to lift up precisely the opposite notion—the notion that we can and ought to give more fucks than ever. The energy of caring is synonymous with empowerment. While the world may frustrate and wound and oppress us into thinking that giving no fucks is the answer, notice how reactionary of a stance that is. It is

[*] With nods to the punk band Angel Hair.

that outdated, disempowered, "I'm doing what I do because you did what you did" model. To care in the face of whatever has been done, whatever has gone on, whatever mess has been made—that's a true choice, a nonreactive choice, an outrageous choice, a self-directed choice, an empowered choice. The energy of caring is not bosh, it is not flimsy. It is, counterintuitively, an expression of strength. To give a fuck is fiery. It takes courage. It requires that we leap from the nest of our comfort zones. To feel cared *for*, after all—that is, to feel that we matter, are respected, listened to, understood, considered, and that our efforts count—is at the heart of all that we want and all that we strive for at the end of the day. It doesn't matter if it's our lover, our coworker, our lawmakers, or our president; it's what we all want. The energy of caring is at the heart of justice itself. And it is at the heart of the emotionally intelligent and transformational processes used throughout this book.

Although we will be exploring a range of practices in this book, at their center is what is commonly referred to as *parts work*. This kind of work, as you'll soon see, asks us to give a damn that we are angry, that we are numb, that we are overthinking, that we are resentful, that we are self-punishing—whatever it is. It sees these emotional experiences as important and meaningful, as opportunities for growth we can't find anywhere else, and—perhaps most importantly—as bridges that can help us connect with the world around us in a healing way. But we must first choose to allow our psycho-emotional experiences to be a cause for curiosity and introspection rather than just another occasion to either self-medicate or go off.

This book is among the first to offer a parts work approach to emotional resilience using examples drawn directly from people's most pressing individual and sociopolitical concerns. My hope is that you will find yourself accessing the insights and practices from *Don't Tell Me to Relax* in all manner of situations—the inner turmoil of self-criticism or social media FOMO, the emotional challenge of constant exposure to brutality through the news (or our neighborhoods), the difficulty of honest and even confrontational conversations with the people in your life. With a little bit of persistence, the perspectives and practices that we're about to dive into can become resources available to you whenever you find yourself in emotionally challenging situations. What's more, my hope is that the insights put forth here will help you disentangle your psycho-emotional world so that you can be more efficacious as you continue to fight for environmental justice, health care, and universal human rights.

It's been said that the personal is the political. I don't think that sums it up at all. *The personal is the political is the spiritual is the emotional is the neuropsychological is the familial is the economic is the interpersonal is the sexual is the societal is the professional.* All threads of our lives form one fabric. Frayed though we may have become, reintegration is not only possible; it's a mission we must endeavor for as if the very survival of our species depends on it. Because it does.

A NOTE REGARDING THE PRACTICES IN THIS BOOK

Like a bicycle, this book rides on two wheels: sections of chapters containing theory, philosophy, and science; and sections of contemplative practices that are informed by the preceding theoretical chapters. This is in keeping with the traditions of meditation wherein potent ideas have always integrated and intertwined with potent inner processes (and vice versa). The two together are meant to form a vehicle that takes one beyond mere musing or intellectual understanding into direct experiences that engender meaningful and abiding change. Thus, you will notice this book alternates between the two, making this a less linear read. One way to use this book, then, would be to read a section of chapters first and then take the time to explore the practices that follow before moving on to the next set of chapters and practices. That said, there are those of you who may want to skip the practices in order to keep reading the theoretical chapters. Or, you might find that you read a chapter, discover something in it you want to go deeper with, skip ahead to the related practice, and then jump back to the theoretical chapters after that. And then there are those of you who will use this book nonsequentially—opening it to whatever chapter or practice is most relevant to you in that moment.

I advocate any of these approaches and hope you trust your own most earnest guidance here. It's a bit like a choose-your-own-adventure novel. Hopefully, one with far fewer dragons and dead ends.

A blanket trigger warning is appropriate here, too. The practices in this book are designed to give you a path and methodology for relating directly to your mind's psychological and emotional content. That content may involve pain, shame, fear, distress, or disturbing memories. In some of these practices, you'll be asked to bring up a memory from childhood or to remember something that angered or frightened you so that you can offer yourself compassion and activate healing energy processes. Only you can judge whether or not it might be useful to engage with such emotional content. If you are someone with a complex past or are particularly sensitive, it may be advisable to tread with caution as you begin such practices, or to skip them until you feel more ready.

Finally, this book is for educational purposes only. Though it discusses and offers advice about mental health, this book should not be used in place of actual therapy. If you are someone with a history of trauma, emotional instability, or mental health diagnoses, please only engage in the practices in this book in collaboration with care from a licensed mental health professional you are working with on an ongoing basis. Please seek professional help immediately if you have thoughts of killing (or otherwise harming) yourself or others, if you are abusing substances, or if you or someone else is in any danger of harm.

Again, we need you. You matter. A lot. So, let's go deep, let's get really real, but please respect your own limits.

PART ONE »
A TIME TO BE FIERY

1 THE PAST IS PRESENT

When the Trauma of Right Now
Intertwines with the Trauma of Yesterday

Mastering the art of resilience does much more than
restore you to who you once thought you were. Rather,
you emerge from the experience transformed into a
truer expression of who you were really meant to be.
—*Carol Osborn*

» I teach about two things: the suffering that comes from
emotional confusion and the freedom that comes from emotional intelligence. My mission on this planet is to help others
discern the nature of our emotional lives—what our emotions
are, why they are, how different emotions dynamically interact with each other, and, most importantly, that how *we*
interact with them is everything. We have a relationship to
each of our many emotional parts, and those relationships
can either bring about a life-altering harmony or deepen a
fog of distortion.

I'm an ideal candidate for the job, really. I've spent most
of my life being upset in one way or another. Ask anyone
who's known me a while, and they'll wince a little bit as they
try to find a polite response. There was a time when all I ever

did was act out my confusion, multiplying the hurt and anger I felt by inflicting it on others and myself. I didn't know how to discern my feelings, how to stop and relate to them, or that I had a choice other than repressing them or letting them rule me. That I became obsessed with how our emotions work and the role they play in our lives is what I've had to do to resist psychic death. My work was born out of necessity—truly, as a means of survival.

In high school, I authored a DIY punk zine called *No Fun*—which was, sadly, not named after the Iggy Pop song (that would've been way cooler). Rather, "no fun" was what my friends constantly said about me. They endlessly reminded me that I was too enraged by racism, sexism, homophobia, and the myriad other forms of bigotry in the world. I was too intense about finding my place within an unjust society, too loud about it all.

Matters of identity have always been complex for me. First of all, I'm biracial. I grew up in a Mexican home with my full-blooded Mexican mom and sisters (who were technically half-sisters, but it never felt that way). That said, the Oklahoman Dutch blood in me is what has always shown through in my light skin. It gets even dicier when I try to pin down gender and sexuality. I was assigned male at birth and have always been comfortable in this male body. Gender identity is another story, though. Presented with the binary of "girls do this, and boys do that," my answer has always been, "Huh?" I identify as a "gender dropout" because no other labels have resonance for me. "Genderqueer," "nonbinary," "gender neutral," . . . I've tried them on and they kindasorta worked, but my true position on the matter is simply, "I don't get it and I don't see why I should have to." In terms of gender *expression*, however, I've been "feminine" as all get-out since birth and have paid dearly for it. Not the least of which were the several confused years when I dated men. My presentation had been mistaken for queerness growing up, and I had been called a fag (etc.) so many times that it blurred the lines of what I knew to be true. And yet the surprise ending for me was discovering that my sexual and romantic affinities belong to those who identify as women only. Which is to say, I walk in the world with straight, white, male privilege . . . and yet, my experience doesn't match what those labels connote. Back in high school, I was figuring out that all of this really mattered but was lost as to how to process my experience.

I was bullied and beaten both in and out of school—penalties paid for my inability (and, at times, outright refusal) to perform normative masculinity. "Why are you so weird?" was forever echoing in my ears. At sixteen, I dropped out of high school and stopped going outside almost entirely for fear of getting jumped again. There was the pain and terror of the violence—that was the obvious part—but then there was also the hidden pain of not being able to understand why I'd been made a target just for not being like other boys. Today, I am thankful to have gone through it all, though. Primarily because I know what happened next.

Radical feminism was my first spiritual awakening. The narratives and theories I found in Riot Grrrl literature and antiestablishment, politically charged punk rock music were, for me, far more than just aesthetic. They named and unpacked my experience of the world with a precision I had never known. In my dawning awareness, I could finally see and describe how bullying came down to power, and how that power was really about safety versus vulnerability. I was being jumped because being a not-particularly-masculine boy made me look vulnerable, and other boys felt compelled to attack me so they could appear invulnerable (lest they become a target like me). This insight dawned as I considered, for the first time, the status and treatment of women in our society. To be able to draw parallels to my own experience helped me to finally feel seen. Meanwhile, to be exposed to the ways in which girls, women, and actual LGBTQAI+ people had it worse was righteously infuriating.

My eyes opened to the reality that my experience was a microcosm of dynamics playing out in innumerable and much more severe ways the world over. Here I was, traumatized to the point of acute isolation, and yet I was still one of the lucky ones. My brain exploded, as I first began to conceive of the abuses that are commonplace in our world. This sociopolitical awakening offered a pressure valve for a kettle on the boil for far too long. And so, my kettle shrieked its message—a message so charged with pent-up emotional energy that no one could hear it. And so, I was told I was overreacting, too dramatic—I needed to relax.

I was No Fun.

My friends were jerks. But it was also true that I ran around biting people's heads off. For example, I would break into tears and scream at audience members at punk shows when I felt a band's message was sexist. The articles in my zine and the lyrics I wrote in my own punk bands were barely coherent. They were appreciated by some, but only those who already felt the same way I did. It was helpful to connect with such kindred spirits, but the anger rarely translated into real action, real organizing—not to speak of actually reaching people outside our small circle.

It's been said that the point of communication is to be heard. I wasn't communicating. I was *expressing.* Both have value, but if you have an important message you think might help change the world, that's a message that needs to be communicated. This isn't to say that activists and change agents ought to water down their messages so as to be palatable to the masses. That's another topic for another book. I want to point us in the direction of a different matter altogether. One that's nearly universal in nature. One that's germane to matters of resilience amid the struggle—to psychological clarity in the realm of psychic death.

I can see something important now that I wasn't capable of seeing back then: the angst I was directing at sociopolitical realities predated me being bullied in school. The way that my outrage regarding racism and xenophobia manifested was very much informed by earlier experiences. My trauma history had begun with people much closer to me. Before I had developed anger at "the system," I had experienced a different, much more intimate kind of system: my family. It'd be many years until I'd understand that my anger about, for instance, the president, was tangled up with anger about another kind of president: my dad. Both angers were valid; that they were tangled up did not negate or dilute either of them. But my emotional situation was unclear and confused, which is a recipe for neither empathic self-understanding nor effective community action.

REWRITING OUR HISTORIES

We've been told "the past is gone," but this is scientifically untrue. The past is right here in our bodies. Research shows that the experiences we accrue are absorbed into our nervous systems, our cells, our fascia. This is especially true of our untended woundings, our unprocessed traumas, the model scenes of our lives (especially from childhood) that communicated more to our psyches than words ever could.

Our emotions are laced with the past. Our attitudes have been molded by yesterday. Our behaviors are most often an amalgam of things that were modeled for us by adults when we were small. And so much of this is held in our unconscious minds and memory systems that inform, to a great extent, our beliefs about what our life is worth, how we handle problems, how relationships work, and how societies operate. But our brains themselves don't know that, just as our eyes cannot turn to see themselves. The past is not gone. The past is who and what we are now.

This is a promising truth. For if the past is not gone, it is not set in stone, either. We can change the way the past lives in our bodies. We can rewire our emotional patterns, and we can even, in deeper therapeutic processes, rewrite memories. We can retrieve parts of us that have been exiled and disavowed. We can mend what is fragmented and disharmonious in us. In this book, I will argue that doing such work is among the highest and most important gifts we can offer ourselves, our families, our communities, and the world.

A Story

CONTENT WARNING: child neglect, drunk driving, and violence

Summertime in Oklahoma. A moment in space and time when my child mind could get lost in simple pleasures. On this evening, the smell of the fresh river air rose up all around me. The sun had just fully set. Swarms of fireflies did not shy away from a full display of their otherworldly magic. The sound of the water rushing by accompanied the lazy swells washing over my small, eight-year-old feet, bare in the maroon sand lining the banks of the Red River.

I wish the story ended there. Moments like these were always haunted by a background of dread. Because if I was in Oklahoma, it was because I was visiting my dad. Which meant things could, and probably would, turn rotten at any moment. My dad was the first of many bullies in my life, and the first of many to invoke mortal fear in me.

My father was an openly abusive, flagrantly racist, abandoner of five children and seven (seven!) marriages—and, to boot, a feverishly proselytizing evangelical Christian through it all. My childhood home vibrated in the wake of his whiplash alcoholic episodes and his attempts to leave us homeless and destitute after his sudden disappearance. He eventually reappeared, living three states away. He invited me to visit, to rekindle the relationship. And kindling is what I got.

On this night at the Red River, my hand was burned in a campfire. Was it a first-degree burn? Second-degree? I don't know because I wasn't taken to a doctor. I went to my dad, panicked, to show him my actively blistering hand and was met by his retort, "What do you want me to do, kiss it and make it better?" His drinking buddies all laughed and went back to playing cards. His kiss-it-and-make-it-better comment amounted to him telling me to relax about a matter that was considerably urgent. And when I couldn't relax, he let me know he thought I was overreacting again, this time in a much more terrifying way.

Though humiliated, I persisted in trying to get him to help me. I *at least* needed ice, and there wasn't any around. My dad caved in. Angrily. What I didn't know was that this meant he would drive us home while black-out drunk. As he sped down a narrow backwoods dirt road, furious with me for disrupting his evening, his pickup truck scraped against a tree. And then another tree. And then another. For fifteen full minutes, I sat frozen stiff, clutching my seat, with every drunk-driving scene I had ever witnessed in movies and TV and educational videos at school flashing through my mind. We sideswiped another tree, and it took the rearview mirror right next to me clean off. I was certain that we were going to die and helpless to do a thing about it.

I'll never forget my dad cracking open a can of Old Milwaukee the next morning, looking out the window, saying, "What the hell happened to my truck?" Never mind what the hell had happened to his son.

Revisiting my dad's reaction to my burned hand all these years later, I'm reminded of the matching T-shirts I saw a smiling couple wearing in 2016. The shirts read "Fuck Your Feelings." The politically charged message was a staunch comment on "snowflakes," a backlash against a generation with their hands in a campfire, trying to figure out what to do. The irony is, there is never a moment when human beings aren't feeling something. Including these folks. "Fuck Your Feelings" is a statement full of feeling. After all, bitterness is a feeling. Coldness is a feeling. Numbness is a feeling. Emotionally shut down is a feeling. Not wanting to deal with feelings is a feeling. The T-shirt wasn't a negation of the importance of feelings. It was actually saying, "Our feelings are the ones that matter." The T-shirt was all about feelings.

This was my dad's attitude toward me at eight years old, and it remained that way until he died. Fuck your feelings. Feelings don't matter. Unless they're mine.

Another Story

Flash forward a decade or so and—big surprise—I'm a drug-addicted drunk reenacting my trauma in one dysfunctional relationship after the next. I want to make sure to say that none of these have resulted in physical violence, as is commonly the case and an active threat for so many.* The story I want to tell you next is about a night that showed me so much about the power of empathy to affect, and even transform, human psychology. It is a story of how another person related to me externally in the exact same way we can relate to ourselves internally.

I was mid-incoherent-argument with a partner. I can't even tell you what we were fighting about. I just remember that in the midst of our exchange of outbursts, I heard her ask me a powerful question:

"What did they *do* to you?"

It stopped me dead in my tracks. I didn't know it, but I had waited my entire life for someone to ask me this question, to be curious about how I came to have a constant thrum of desperation in my life. My entire body softened. I began weeping. Memories of violence flashed in my mind's eye. My dad's earth-shattering shout. The night a gun was held to my head. Another night when a knife was held to my ribs. The night they beat my best friend with a pipe. The night another "friend" screamed in my face, "Just admit that you're a faggot already so I can beat the shit out of you now."

And yet, in this moment, I was grateful. Grateful that someone could tell something was done to me. Someone saw through the veil of my reactivity to the terrible and unacknowledged experiences I had internalized. To the way my past was present. Someone wanted to know how life had come to be such a painfully twisted-up mess. *What did they do to*

---

* I also want you to know that dysfunctions in intimacy have been an enormous motivation in my ongoing trauma-focused inner work and process, which has included making amends for situations like the one I'm about to describe.

me? Certainly, it hadn't always been this way. Oddly enough, I didn't even need to tell her about any of it at that point. Neither of us said anything more. Being asked was somehow enough on its own.

We were on our way to sleep when I finally said, "Thank you."

"For what?"

"For your question. For asking what they had done to me."

"Oh. That's not what I said. I asked, 'What the hell is wrong with you?'"

I had misheard her.

I got up, got in my car, and drove home. Drunk.

My father's son keeping the family tradition.

2 THE WISDOM OF AN ENRAGED GODDESS

Learning to Trust Our Anger

What matters most is how well
you walk through the fire.
—*Charles Bukowski*

» **HER** skin is the blue-black of ravens. Her hair is matted, wild. Her tongue is dripping with blood. Around her neck hangs a garland of skulls she's kept as trophies. Around her waist, a skirt of severed arms. There is no question regarding your fate should you cross her. Best to stay on her good side. In one hand, she holds a sword. In the other, she holds the decapitated head of her latest conquest. She is a destroyer, a marauder, a rebel of the highest order. She is the most powerful being the universe has known. Her rage knows no bounds. She goes shrieking into the night.

And yet she is not evil. She is no demon. She is, in the Vedic traditions, a high and holy being. It's taught that her rage is imbued with goodness, with wisdom. Her sword represents the cutting, penetrating nature of capital-T Truth. The heads she's cut off represent objectification, cruelty, and greed. Her only enemy is dehumanization. Her compassion is so great, so boundless, so far-reaching that she is willing to confoundingly manifest in a grotesque form as a display of it. She is Ma Kali, literally, the "Mother of Time." And she is most revered by many.

You might ask how divinity could be represented in this way. Or why anyone would embrace such a dichotomy. If we get to know the horrifically exquisite Kali better, we'll see why.

Kali has many origin stories, but I'll tell you the version I love most. She came into being at a time of unprecedented, widespread crisis. A demon-god named Mahisasura had obtained miraculous powers and intended to enslave all beings. His powers had become greater than that of Lord Brahma, who created the entire cosmos with a single exhale; greater than that of Lord Vishnu, who effortlessly maintains the very fabric of existence; greater than that of Lord Shiva, whose cosmic dance calls all beings toward transformation, death, and rebirth. Mahisasura, intoxicated by his newfound powers, gathered an army of demons in order to unseat the Brahma-Vishnu-Shiva trinity so that he could set out to wreak havoc for beings everywhere.

Brahma, Shiva, and Vishnu gathered the other gods: Yama, the god of death; Chandra, the goddess of the moon; Agni, the god of fire; and all the rest came together. Not one of them was powerful enough to stop Mahisasura on their own . . . and they were angry—angry at the destruction that was to ensue, angry at the immense suffering to come. Their collective anger became so great that it spontaneously emanated as light and heat from the space between each of their eyebrows. From their third eyes, from the light and heat of their anger, the mighty and terrible Kali came into form. Without hesitation, she laid waste to Mahisasura and his army, adorning herself with their remains—their skulls and limbs. This was both in the spirit of victory as well as to set fear in the hearts of any other evil beings who might attempt to challenge her. Kali for the win. The biggest win in the history of the material universe.

Kali's story is that of a powerful spiritual being vanquishing sociopolitical injustice. After all, what are Brahma, Vishnu, and Shiva presiding over the very universe if not a government? And a demonic god attempting a coup d'état that would put the lives and well-being of countless beings in peril—this is a deeply sociopolitical matter. There are, of course, many other implications. This story also contains a silent sermon to those soaking in self-judgment because our anger is "bad vibes" or, in Buddhism, "one of the three poisons," and thus categorically wrong. Yet, because Kali's aim was so pure and so just (an important point), she could just let her anger run loose. Beyond unabashed, she adorned herself with the limbs of the slain, trophies of her holy rampage. This offers another implicit message. If we struggle with feeling less than conventionally beautiful, if we struggle with feeling less than "lovable," if we struggle with others misunderstanding us—Kali represents all of those things, too. She's a not-hot mess and yet she is the aggregated energies of all the highest beings in the heavens. She is the epitome of a beauty in the raw, uncorrupted by commercialism.

We conceive of spirituality, compassion, and well-being as solemn and quiet affairs. Kali reminds us that such interpretations are far too one-dimensional. She reminds us that sacred and altruistic action can take just about any form. If handled right, the entire spectrum of human experience is worthy fodder for transformation.

✦ ✦ ✦

Just as we could use more English words for love in order to express the many forms love takes, we need more words for anger. So many are its shapes and shades. Bewildering, almost all of them. But I cannot underline this point enough: anger almost never operates without some form of logic behind it. Anger is almost never random. It has intelligence. There is the anger that tells us a boundary needs to be set. There is the rage that guards an old wound within us. There is the outrage we feel on behalf of someone else who has been wronged. There is the resentment we hold in our bones for apologies we're likely to never get. Then there is the quick, staccato arising of insult when we feel disregarded in some way.

And yet, all angers have but one source: they are rooted in compassion. Anger is always a response to hurt, to our basic needs for safety and belonging. Its very purpose is to address hurt in some way. That's why anger exists *at its onset*, and that makes it quite synonymous with the energy of compassion. Anger is, every time, a powerful vital force that is birthed to right perceived wrongs, to restore safety, to address the unspeakable. And it is powerful so that we'll have the energy to follow through, ideally restoring relative safety and respect.

Equating anger and compassion may sound preposterous because we don't experience anger that way on the surface. We have plenty of examples of being hurt by the unleashing of anger, both our own and others'. Anger might have a good root, but its expression so often takes the form of aggression. Vengeful. Tense. Eclipsing all reason. It's as if the initial compassionate energy of anger passes through a thousand filters of cultural, social, and familial conditioning before it arrives in our conscious awareness. You might even notice that the angrier parts of you resemble people in your family—that the "voice" inside you when you're pissed off sounds like your father, mother, sister, brother, or someone else who mattered to you growing up. Such emotional patterns are often passed down through bloodlines.

When an angry part of us takes over, it's as if we become a different person. Our thoughts change, our words change, we become capable of things we'd ordinarily find reprehensible. In anger, we ourselves become capable of betraying someone's basic needs for safety and belonging, capable of hurting others. It's the worst irony in existence, that what starts out as strong desire to address perceived harm so often ends up causing harm. A painful cycle that has the wish for an end to pain at its core. As the saying goes, "Hurt people hurt people."

Looking through the lens of the "static paradigm" of emotions I mentioned at the beginning of this book, we objectify our anger as a big problem and objectify ourselves as an "angry person." Looking through the lens of the emotional "process paradigm" I mentioned in the introduction, we could identify our anger as the expression of part of us that has been activated for a reason, by the situation we're in (which very well may be reminding us of a historical situation in which we were traumatized). We can start to see that the angry part of us is like another person or being who deeply wishes to right wrongs but is stricken with a shortsightedness of the heart. Beginning to see our anger as another person who lives inside of us can be a key to breaking the trance of that anger. This shift in perception can open the door to taking a breath—a breath, followed by a mental step backward from the flood of feeling. I suggest this not so we can rid ourselves of that flood or fix it or "make it more spiritual." The idea, rather, is to remember that we are more than this feeling, this fire—we are also the mind, heart, and body that gets to choose what to do with it.

What would it be like if we could help the angry part of us find an expression closer to its inner truth—closer to its altruistic, helpful, valuable nature? What would it be like to check in with our anger and ask if it really wants to be this way or if it feels like it *must* be this way?

I wonder if the angry parts of you are actually exhausted. I wonder if they feel like they're trapped in a cycle. It must be so much work, generating all that adrenaline and heat and furious thinking. If we continue with the view that an angry part of us is like its own being, then it is definitely a being who feels awful constantly. Anger is, after all, among the most hellish feelings we can experience. And yet, following this logic, this is a being who is willing to live in that hellish place in order to protect us, in order to stand up for what we believe is right. Seeing things in this way, it starts to dawn on us that anger is an energy within us that deserves our appreciation.

It's time to stop being afraid of our anger and shoving it aside as if it has no value, and it is also time to stop being intoxicated by our anger. We can learn to take a step back from our inner Kalis and offer them some appreciation. Strangely enough, in offering compassion to angry parts of us, those parts just might be freed to move closer to their original, compassionate nature.

3

EMOTIONAL ALCHEMY

Skills for Using Fire without Getting Burned

No feeling is final.
—*Rainer Maria Rilke*

» **BACK** to the days when I was No Fun.

Like Kali, I was (and am) angry about the systemic, cruel treatment of other living beings. Like Kali, I saw (and still see) forces in this world rising up that intentionally push lives that matter into the margins where they are derailed and destroyed. Like Kali, my natural impulse is to do what I can to end all forms of abuse. Unlike Kali, however, I have a trauma history. Unlike Kali, we *all* have trauma histories, to a greater or lesser extent, and those histories have conditioned where our awareness goes, what stands out to us, and the ways our hearts respond. All of which is to say, unlike Kali, I don't exist in a supernatural state wherein I can act on the impulse of my anger free of emotional intoxication. (Hopefully it goes without saying that the mythos of Kali is not meant to be taken literally—it's not giving us permission to go on a murderous rampage.) The mythos of Kali has much to show us about the ultimate nature of anger; it is here to expand our view. It reminds me that I can indeed welcome anger as my friend. This in turn helps me to be less enmeshed in it, which then helps me to not lose sight of the compassionate spark at the root of my anger.

Reading Kali's origin story can give us inspiration to recover the energy of compassion within a moment of anger. The story itself doesn't show us how to enact that recovery, but in this book I'll be sharing simple inner processes that can achieve that result. We'll be trying some of these processes out in the practices section that follows this chapter, as a conclusion to part 1 of this book, and then we'll do more practices at the end of the other parts of the book. But let's try a little sampler right now.

A PRELIMINARY INTRODUCTION TO PARTS WORK

Although I won't be explaining the concepts and theories embedded in this practice until later in this chapter and in subsequent chapters, this exercise already contains aspects of all the important practices we'll be exploring throughout the book. I encourage you to return to it at any time. Also, this exercise is most appropriate for working with feelings that are somewhat neutral, such as the way we feel when we are reading and processing information or going about our day-to-day tasks. We will get to working with the deeper layers soon enough.

Bring your attention to what's going on with you emotionally and cognitively as you read. Bring some attention to the body; does your mental state seem to be affecting you physically (or vice versa)? Pause and close your eyes for a moment, and see if there's tension in the jaw, heaviness in the chest, knots in the stomach, or something else. Or maybe you're too up in your head to do that kind of noticing right now. If so, then "listen" for a moment to your thoughts. What are they saying? What are the themes? Are there laundry lists being made? Memories bubbling up? Do you feel a sudden urge to be doing something else? Maybe there's an effort to get this exercise "right." It's very likely that the parts of you that are present are trying to help you in some way, such as trying to figure something out, reminding you of things you need to do, resisting the unknown territory of this exercise, or reminding you that you need to do better in some way.

In noticing this about the sensations or "voices" inside of us, we're engaging in something called *unblending*—a concept I describe later in this chapter.[2] For now, notice that there are at least two aspects of your being present—an aspect expressing feelings and thoughts, and an aspect noticing those feelings and thoughts.

Now I want you to try something you may have never done before: see if you can find a space inside where it's possible to get a little bit curious about these parts of yourself. What are they up to? Why do they make the mind so active? Is there an agenda here? It might help to take a few conscious breaths first. Then, once you feel a friendly sense of wanting to know a bit more, try expressing curiosity inside yourself. You could silently say, "I'd like to know more about you. Is there anything you want me to know?" And then just hang out and wait for a few moments.

Generally speaking, when we do this, something happens. You might have gotten more information. You might have gone blank. It might have felt like a bit of a shock. You might have felt like parts of you wanted nothing to do with you. Maybe a memory popped up. Maybe a part of you screamed, "This is stupid!" But something happened. You received a response. Whereas before you might have thought of your thoughts as an "inner monologue," now you've initiated something different—an inner dialogue.

SHIFTING THE INNER DIALOGUE

Generally speaking, our emotions and thoughts can carry us in one of two directions. As they did for me in high school, they can take us to a place where we deepen suffering. But we can also relate to our mind-state in a particular way, such as getting curious about, or even compassionate toward, the troublesome energies within us. When we effect such a shift, we open up the possibility of entering into processes with our emotional and cognitive parts that bring our inner world into harmony. The difference lies in how we interact with them. Many of us don't know that we can interact with our psychological parts—much less that we can do so to incredibly promising ends. Our sense is that our feelings are final, and hence there's no point in opening a conversation with them. But they're not final. As Walt Whitman famously wrote, "I am large, I contain multitudes." We are not one-dimensional, and our multiple dimensions are not static. Just as our bodies are made of many parts that form a dynamic, interwoven system that works together, so it is with our psyches. We are more awake, alive, and complex than we know.

Maybe my story about how I was treated and how I reacted in high school seems extreme to you, or maybe it sounds like a walk in the park compared to your teenage years. The point is, we've all been wounded to a greater or lesser degree, and this leads us to develop patterns of defense. For me, I used to become so eclipsed by my defensive anger that I'd collapse into a certain hatred of the world, into an existential bitterness about humanity and life itself. Even though my anger was trying to keep me safe by urging me to recoil from the world, because I had no conscious *relationship* to my anger, no process for talking to it and clarifying it, my anger ended up exacerbating my trauma and depression and causing harm. In the depths of my repeat depressive episodes, my belief that people were no good and that I was no good left me highly prone to lashing out. As this naturally pushed people away from me, my belief that people were no good and that I was no good would be confirmed and reconfirmed, taking me further into the depths, which made me even more prone to lashing out . . . and down the spiral I'd go.

This is the emotional confusion I spoke of in chapter 1. My relationship to my grief and rage was such that I was either taken over by it or I'd exert tremendous amounts of energy pushing it into a dark corner where no one could see it. I'd either be intoxicated by it—which meant it dictated my thoughts, words, and actions—or I'd self-medicate with entertainment or substances. This, in turn, impacted both my outer world, where I became increasingly isolated and misunderstood, and my inner world, where I felt increasingly hopeless and stuck.

Yet, I did eventually discover the emotional intelligence that I spoke of in chapter 1: processes that helped me evolve my relationship to anger so that it owned me less and less. How was it that the spiral eventually reversed? Here is part of the wisdom of our so-called negative emotions—they are expert at getting our attention. Anger made my life such a mess that it eventually gave me no choice but to turn around and do the work to heal. In this way, difficult emotions beckon us toward alchemy.

That dysfunctional fight I had with my partner offers a big clue as to how this alchemy can happen. In the midst of conflict, I heard her ask a simple but powerful question: *"What* *did they do to you?"** It stopped me dead in my tracks, cut right through my anger, and opened the door to a healing that my nervous system desperately needed. I perceived curiosity and empathy in her question, which were like essential nutrients I was starved for at the time. The angry part of me that was front and center suddenly softened, clearing space for something much more tender in me to emerge. The question implied "What happened for you to become this person who's this upset all the time? It couldn't have always been like this." Curiosity and compassion are indeed powerful energies.

Imagine that you're in a tense conversation with someone—a partner, friend, coworker, family member, or even a stranger—(to be clear, one where actual abuse or violence isn't present or imminent) and you somehow find the mental space to ask a curious and empathic question. At least two other things would have to happen to make that possible. First, you'd have to pause. You'd have to drop out of the conversation for a moment, even if only mentally. Second, you'd have to take a step back from your own anger and hurt in order to flip the emotional script toward generosity. And while you might ask, "Why would I ever do that if someone's coming at me the wrong way?" I must point out, in the instance with my partner, it *stopped* me from continuing to come at her the wrong way.

We can literally do the same thing within ourselves. We can move from the kind of monologue that comes from believing that our feeling is final to a dialogue of empathic inner communication. Doing so changes everything, but usually it requires a few simple skills. Without further ado, these skills are as follows:

---

* It doesn't matter at all that, in that moment, I only *thought* I had heard that question—the brain runs on perception, not actualities.

1. Pause.
2. Unblend.
3. Get curious.
4. Shift the inner conversation.

Let's look at them one by one.

The Power of Pause

To pause is to reclaim our attention. It's to reel ourselves back in. It's to come back to our senses—literally. It's to come back to being in our bodies.

This deceptively simply skill is quite revolutionary. Your attention is one of the most sought-after commodities on the planet. About $200 billion a year is spent by the data-mining industry trying to figure out how to capture your attention, distract you, and make you feel whatever way an advertiser or political org wants you to feel.[3] So, in a world that screams "Look at this! Buy this! Do more! We don't care if it's killing you! We don't care if it's ruining the entire planet and everyone on it!" learning how to reclaim our attention is a necessary act of resisting psychic death. If we are to remain psychologically free, questioning, perceptive, sovereign beings, then we must continually recalibrate our minds around our deeper intentions.

The key to learning how to pause in the midst of difficult and intense emotions is to begin pausing periodically throughout the day at times when you're *not* triggered. Check in with yourself at least as much as you check Instagram. Stay in touch with your inner world at least as much as you keep abreast of the outer world. Binge-watch your well-being. Decide you want to fully show up as an embodied, liberated, emotionally bright, spiritually connected person as you do all the things. You are a fascinating being of enormous capacity.

"Having all the feels" doesn't even begin to describe it. A cosmos filled with big bangs and black holes and supernovas and nebulae is churning inside you. Many people go their whole lives without noticing this, much less basking in it. Among many other worthy things, pausing is about making sure that not-noticing doesn't happen to us—making sure not to squander what the poet Mary Oliver called our "one wild and precious life."

Unblending

Imagine you're standing in front of a painting you really want to see. Except you're standing one inch away from it. You can't see it. You're too close. There's not enough space for you to appreciate what's right in front of you. Naturally, you'd want to take a few steps back. Not because you're trying to get away from the painting—in fact, just the opposite. You step back because you want to see it more clearly. You want to see all of it.

When we stand too close to our strong emotions, we become them. We get overridden, hijacked. We *blend* with them. In this state, our options are few. We get tunnel vision. We lose context. We say things we don't mean. We do things one part of us thinks we need to do in order to protect ourselves, but then, later, another part of us regrets it. We're in our emotions but somehow not connected to them. Paradoxically, it's when we *unblend*—that is, when we take two steps back from our emotions—that we can best understand them and honor the messages they have for us. Unblending simply means putting a little space, a little daylight, between ourselves and the emotional parts of us that are activated.

You might think that your emotions are sometimes too intense for you to do this. The truth is, the more intense the emotion, the more we must find that space if we are to avoid hurting ourselves or others. The more gripping the feeling state, the more awareness we need to bring to the situation and the more urgent it is that we pause, breathe, and regain our center before taking even one more step.

Unblending is a way of reclaiming your agency in moments when you feel triggered. Once you're unblended, you can begin connecting to aspects of your deeper wisdom without having to judge or disavow the triggered parts of you.

Getting Curious

When you stop and get curious about your emotional state, you can listen more clearly to the feeling, respond to the feeling, reason with the feeling, bring compassion to the feeling. You can decide whether the feeling is something you'd really like your actions to be informed by (or not). You can also shift the conversation you're having within yourself. Which then means you can shift the conversation you're having with others—it's much easier, after all, to tell someone how you're feeling if you have enough distance from your feelings to be able to communicate your experience accurately.

When we open to curiosity, we are that much closer to our natural state of childlike wonder. When we touch curiosity, we graze the rim of infinite possibility. To become curious, genuinely curious, about our situation is to invite movement into what was once stuck and fraught. It is to bring warmth into an experience without having to ask that experience to change. There's something mysterious about the moment curiosity comes trickling into a struggle within ourselves. Our parts, of course, may fight it and block it for some time. But once they themselves feel it and relent, the paradigm shift is undeniable.

Curiosity is entry-level compassion, entry-level caring. In moments when having compassion (for ourselves or someone else) feels either out of reach or wholly unreasonable, curiosity is much easier to access. It's entry-level compassion because when we get curious and inquisitive, we are on our way to understanding things in a new way. The more we understand where a part of us is coming from, the more likely compassion and caring are to spontaneously dawn.

When Curiosity Is Blocked

When troublesome or pained parts of us are present, it's common for other parts to come in and judge, resist, shut down, or analyze the situation. For example, a client might say to me, "I can't get curious about my anger right now because I hate it so much." To which I'd honestly respond, "Of course you do. Anger is uncomfortable and makes messes. I get why another part of you hates it." People often find the next step utterly surprising. We can ask the part of us that's judging the angry part to relax and step to the side. We simply acknowledge the judging part in a friendly way and ask if it'd be willing to relax a bit. Amazingly, this works. And when it doesn't—if, for example, the judging part won't step aside—we simply switch to working with the judging part instead, get curious about it, and go from there.

This will work with numbness, with distractedness, with all kinds of parts of us. Sometimes people will say to me, "I can't do parts work because I feel so shut down inside." But that shut down feeling is coming from a part of them. So, we pause, get curious about the experience of "shut down inside," and then move to the next step.

If this seems confusing, don't worry. Just keep going. With enough friendly observation, the architecture of the mind is sure to reveal itself organically.

Shifting the Conversation Inside

Having paused, unblended, and gotten curious (all of which can happen in an instant once we've built the habit), we are now in a position to ask questions that come from the energy of that curiosity. Is this a part of you that's weighed down by a wound or betrayal of some sort? Or is it a part of you that's come to protect you in some way? What emotions are present? Do you feel them in the body? If so, where? And what are the sensations like? Heavy or light? Sharp or dull? Pulsing or constant? More warm or more cool? Does this part of you have a "voice?" If so, what are they saying? Or maybe you start getting images when you get curious. If so, what are they? And are they related to historical moments in your life? I'll be offering many more questions we can use to begin engaging our inner parts in the practices to come, but hopefully it's becoming apparent by now that there is much more going on with our minds and emotions than we've been taught to think there is. What could easily be labeled and dismissed as "sadness" is richer and more multidimensional than that. Getting curious about our feeling of sadness, to follow the example, we can turn inward to find a part of us—a subpersonality, if you will—that has a function, a voice, sensory dimensions, visual dimensions, a history, and even layers of other emotions. All this from what's been a cursory exploration so far. As we continue, we'll find that there's even more to the story.

INSIDE OUT

These steps that enable us to organize an inner dialogue of empathic self-communication—pausing, unblending, getting curious, and using questions for self-inquiry—can be found, with variations and different names, in a number of spiritual and wellness practices. The language I'm using here comes from the parts work process central to IFS. Perhaps the coolest thing about parts work is that it can be practiced without a therapist present. It can be brought into meditation and contemplative practices, and it can be practiced in quick and meaningful ways throughout the day.

Perhaps you've seen or heard of the Pixar movie *Inside Out*. In that movie, all the emotional parts of a little girl named Riley are running around trying to help her navigate daily life in the midst of her parent's separation, and each of those parts has its own job and its own agenda. Quite often those agendas don't match, and the parts clash with one another. Isn't it just like that with us sometimes? In fact, the progenitors of IFS have been commissioned as consultants by Pixar in the making of the sequel.

PART ONE PRACTICES

» When You Encounter Horrible Headlines

Consider the last horrible headline you read. It would be best if it weren't something so close to home that you boil over and get furious about it. Pick something somewhat manageable. If you can't think of a headline, recall a situation wherein you felt distressed or angry. Let the emotional parts involved in the experience get activated.

Once one or more emotional parts are present, pause. Take a breath and notice the emotional and cognitive qualities here, and whether you already feel caught up in them. Can you label the primary emotion(s), like "sadness," "worry," or "anger"? Are there sensations in the body such as tight shoulders, knots in the stomach, lower back pain, or something else? Don't try to fix the sensations or make them go away; just feel into them. Notice the "voice" of this part or parts of you, and any associated thoughts. Don't try to shut them out or talk back; just listen and receive them.

Notice that this is a part of you that is responding to the headline in a way that makes sense. There's actually a logic being followed here. This part of you is either wanting to find a way to address the situation, to make things okay again, or it's wounded and deflated in some way in response to something that matters. Even if the experience of its expression feels uncomfortable, this part of you does have an intelligence to it.

Can you take a few breaths now and find a sense of space between you and the emotion? It doesn't have to be a dramatic shift. And, again—importantly—we're not trying to push this part of you away. We just want to get to know it a little, to understand where it's coming from. To do that, we'll need just a little bit of space. Take your time.

Next, see if you can find some curiosity about the activated part of you. Not so much the story of why you feel this, or if you think this part of you is right or wrong, but the experience of it directly—again, the sensations in the body, the things this part of you seems to be saying: "I hate this," "It's not fair," "It can't be this way," or whatever the message might be. See if you can find a space inside where it's possible to find some curiosity or interest about this emotional part of you. Stop there for a moment.

If it's impossible to get curious about that part of you, simply ask all other parts of you if they'll kindly relax and step aside. You may have to do this two or three times before curiosity can dawn. But all you need is a sliver of curiosity, an iota of space.

Notice how you feel now that you're curious about what's happening inside of you, as opposed to being consumed by it, wanting to get rid of it, or being so focused on the external (headline or interaction) that you aren't even aware of your inner feeling. It's as if you're mixing these two together: curiosity and sadness; curiosity and worry; curiosity and whatever it is you're feeling. If you are genuinely curious toward the part of you expressing feelings and thoughts, they might still be there, but notice if you're in a little bit of a better place.

If you'd like to go deeper and (this is important) curiosity, spaciousness, or compassion is present toward this part of yourself, below are some empathic questions you could ask. Don't try to figure out the answers. Just ask and maybe even let the answer surprise you a bit:

» Is there something you'd like me to know?
» Are these feelings connected to something more personal?

» What role are you playing in my life? What job are you trying to do?

» How long have you had that job?

» Do you like doing that job, or is it exhausting?

» If you didn't have to protect me in this way and you could have any other job in the world, what would you rather be doing?

This is one of many ways we can be real about our emotions without being lost in them or avoidant of them.

If you want to take this one step further and find out more about the vulnerability inside you that this reactive part is protecting, you could ask:

» If you stopped protecting me like this, what do you think would happen?

The answer we sense to this question points us in the direction of what is longing to be healed in our lives. Hold that part of you in a place of compassion. You can even use the next practice to offer it some healing energy.

» Self-Love for a Part of You That Needs It Most

Take a few deep breaths and feel what it's like to be in your body. Then, think about a time in childhood when things were relatively simple (even if it was just for a fleeting moment). Begin to get curious about that moment. What age were you then? What grade were you in at school? What were some of the playful things you loved doing then? Can you see what your face looked like at the time? Perhaps you can think of your image from a family photo or a school photo. Can you hear your child voice, your child laugh? It might help to close your eyes for a moment to make the image of your child self more real. Bring that kid right into the room, right here with you.

Then, imagine surrounding your younger self in the energy of your curiosity. See if you can let that curiosity deepen into empathy or even caring. Offer your child self the good vibes you would offer any small child who'd been left in your care. (Even if you don't like kids, you and I both know that if a little kid were left in your care, you'd at least show them some basic kindness.) Extend this energy to them.

Send them some sincere wishes for their well-being. Send them the thoughts, "May you be happy. May you feel safe. May you feel free." Repeat these slowly at least a few times, and imagine the energy of those words reaching them, lighting up their little face. You can send the words on your breath, imagine them as a beam of light, or use any other technique that helps you get there.

You might feel nothing at first, or you might feel a dramatic shift of some sort. Either way, just keep going.

Next, think about a time in childhood when things were difficult. (Note: please don't choose to work with a deeply traumatic memory unless you are highly experienced with self-work of this nature.) Perhaps a memory has been stirring in you as you've been reading. If difficult feelings come up for you right away, practice pausing, unblending, and getting curious. What age were you then? What grade were you in at school? Can you see your child self-image? Can you remember your laugh, your smile? What did it feel like to be you during that time in your life? Perhaps you're having a very specific memory and can see or feel into a whole scene that unfolded for you. Remember or imagine as much as you can about this particular moment in your life. You may need to pause, unblend, and get curious again here.

Extend the energy of curiosity, friendliness, goodwill, or compassion to this kid. Surround them with it. You may want to place a hand on your heart and make sure they know that you're right here with them. If you're feeling emotions in the body such as a heaviness in the chest or a tightness in the throat, it might help to place a compassionate hand there with the same message.

Sometimes it can seem like your inner child part isn't receptive to your care. It's as if this part of you isn't used to receiving such goodness from others, or even from you, and they might not trust it. If that happens, know that this is common and will change over time. Sometimes we need to make amends with our parts for how things have been until now. Sometimes we just need to gently continue wishing them well regardless of their reaction. Like an untrusting cat beginning to realize you have treats for them, they'll eventually come around.

Stay here for a while, holding any feelings that are present in the space of compassion. Conclude by taking five deep cleansing breaths. Make sure to breathe bigger than any of the feelings that have been present in this practice. Make sure to transition gently from this practice and to take amazing care of yourself today.

» When Thoughts Scream: The Self-Love Approach to Calming Inner Critics and Overwhelm

When our thoughts scream, it's a response to a perception of vulnerability. Whether that vulnerability is real or imagined, conscious or unconscious, doesn't matter. Our nervous systems take no chances when it comes to survival; they respond to *any* kind of vulnerability as a matter of survival. You might want to get these inner voices and feelings to shut the hell up, but there's a better way, a way that's rooted in self-love. And it's simple. I just need you to suspend your disbelief while you check out something new, do it at least twice, and then check to see if it worked after you've made those earnest attempts.

Follow these steps:

1. Consider the source of this overwhelm to be another person—or people, as the case may be.
2. Listen to what's being said. Stop trying to push these parts of you away or change them at all. Pause and listen. What are the complaints here? What do these parts of you fear is going to happen? What do they think you did wrong? Listen passively to every last complaint, every last insult.
3. Reflect back what you've heard. Inside yourself (not out loud), repeat back all the complaints you've heard. Every last one. For example: "Okay, I hear that you think I'm garbage, that we're going to fail, that everything is terrible . . ." Some people's voices say very difficult things about aspects of their social identity, like skin color or gender expression. If this happens for you, simply reflect back these sentiments as well. Don't add anything. Just let this part of you know that you hear them.
4. After you've repeated back every complaint, ask inside if there's more. We want to know *all* the complaints. Another good question to ask these parts of you is, "Am I getting it?"
5. If there are more complaints, reflect those back again just like you did in step 3.

6. In your own words and in a kind tone, say to these parts of you, "Now I've heard every complaint—and I get it. I get why you're upset. But, now that I'm hearing and understanding you, do you think you could turn down the volume here? Could you bring the intensity down a bit so that I can have the space to do something about it?"
7. If the complaints persist, it's because there's still more on the table *or* these parts of you don't feel like you've sufficiently heard or understood them. No one continues to scream if they feel truly heard and understood. Repeat steps 1–6.
8. If the complaints still persist, ask inside what these parts of you need from you in order to calm down. Do they need you to set a boundary? To make a change or make some sort of commitment?

Nine times out of ten, raging thoughts and feelings such as these are defensive parts of us. Doing this process, I sometimes (but not always) find that people start feeling vulnerable, emotional, or like a wound inside of them has become present. If this is you, don't be thrown off by it. What you're feeling now is the wounded part(s) of you that were being defended, the more hidden layers of yourself that it would likely feel intolerable should anyone hurt, betray, terrorize, insult, or shame now again. If that's where you are now, with a vulnerable part of you exposed, here are some additional steps for relating inside yourself in a compassionate way.

1. Pause. Unblend. Get curious about what or who is now present inside you. Please don't push them away or try to make them relax. There's been enough of that already. See if, instead, you can find a space inside where you feel open or even caring toward this part of you.

2. If you can't find such a space inside, that's okay. Notice the parts of you that are averse to this wounded part in some way. In a friendly manner, simply ask those other parts to step aside so you can help this troubled part of you. You may have to do this multiple times. Continue until you can find even a tiny space within that's open and clear, perhaps even warm toward the wounded part of you.

3. Explore this part of you a bit by noticing what they're like inside. Are they in the body someplace? What are the sensations? Can you label the primary emotion that's here? Do they have a voice?

4. Once you're able to be curious and maybe even caring, extend that curiosity and caring through the following steps:

> » Simply stay there, as if you're holding or hanging out with that part of you. Just breathe and be there with no agenda whatsoever.
>
> » Ask this part if there's anything they want you to know.
>
> » Place a compassionate hand wherever you feel them in the body (or on the heart center) and say to them, "I'm here. We're safe now. We survived."
>
> » If you have a visual of this part of you, you can offer them things like a blanket or a puppy to help them calm down and feel safe.
>
> » You can return to the first step, simply staying there and breathing, at any time.

AFTERCARE INSTRUCTIONS

There's a solid chance these opening practices got deeper than you thought they would when we started out. If you've gone to a deep place with yourself today, make sure to treat yourself and be extra gentle as you proceed. Some ideas:

1. Call a friend or a family member who's got your back.
2. Take a hot bath (with salts and oils if you have those) or a shower, and wash it all away.
3. Go outside and look up at the sky. Feel how that automatically drops your center of gravity down to your feet.
4. Take five deep breaths and breathe as big as any of the emotions that have been here.
5. Indulge in a simple pleasure such as chocolate or a ridiculous animal video online.
6. Do the "Grounding: Body of Breath" practice on page 94, or go to my website and try one of the breathwork practices there (at www.ralphdelarosa.com/meditations).

Whatever you do, be good to you. Always.

A TIME TO BE TENDER

4 WHAT THE SELF-LOVE MOVEMENT IS MISSING

Awakening from the distortion of oppression begins
with tenderness: we recognize our own wounded
tenderness, which develops into the tenderness of
vulnerability and culminates in the tenderness that
comes with heartfelt and authentic liberation.
—*Zenju Earthlyn Manuel*

CONTENT WARNING: physical assault and childhood
psychological abuse

» GOOGLE search: "What is self-love?"

Therapy blog: "Self-love is knowing your worth and not
settling for less than you deserve."

Self-help blog: "Self-love is embracing the past, present,
and future."

Style blog: "Self-love means you wake up in the morning
with an enthusiastic, positive attitude!"

For Bruce, the idea of waking up ready to face the day with
a positive attitude was inconceivable. Through no fault of
his own, each day began with a tremendous anxiety that was

always with him. And he couldn't embrace his past; his past, on the contrary, was already gripping *him* far too tightly. His past had left him with an unavoidable sense that the world is a dangerous place. His defensive parts had gone haywire, overrode his will, and kept his guard up day and night. This meant dropping out of college, staying in jobs he didn't care for, keeping his social world small, and steering clear of intimate relationships. Bruce was settling for less than he deserved because to go for more felt terrifying.

I met Bruce seven years after he was physically assaulted while asleep in his bedroom. The vicious attack had left a nearly indelible imprint on him. It sent a strong message to his nervous system that if he could be put in life-threatening circumstances while asleep in his own home, then nowhere was safe. His incessant anxiety made sure he had the energy for the arduous task of constantly bracing—scanning his environment for possible threats, scanning his memory for all the things he did and said wrong. Underneath the anxiety lay deep feelings that he had brought the assault on himself, that he was unlovable and unworthy of good things, and that no one would ever really be there for him.

While Bruce's story and experiences are specific to him, I am struck by the universality of the presence of such underlying feelings and beliefs. How many of us, regardless of what it is we've been through, feel unworthy and abandoned, don't believe we deserve good things, or live with an underlying sense that the other shoe is always about to drop? How many of us have done a fair amount of work at improving our lives yet have taken on models of "self-love" that entail shutting down the parts of ourselves that feel unworthy? So many people carry an idea of self-love that involves giving our inner critics the middle finger and walling off painful memories in the name of maintaining a positive attitude.

When we see that such negative beliefs are held by parts of us that are in pain or are reacting to times when love was withheld from us, we start discerning that this approach is actually self-abuse. At best, it's a conditional form of self-love, and conditional love isn't love—it's a transaction. We've been abandoning parts of us that already feel abandoned and beating up on parts of us that already feel beat up. When we pause, unblend, and get curious about the parts of us that are stuck in pain, reactivity, and negative self-beliefs, we offer them exactly what they've been missing all along.

Though in my examples above I'm throwing shade at the Google-results version of teachings on self-love, the self-love movement isn't wrong in its basic orientation. I'm a huge fan of self-love, but a lot of the approaches to it that I've encountered are incomplete. What the self-love movement is missing is techniques regarding how we can get to feelings of love, positive regard, and harmonious alliance within ourselves *without* attacking, repressing, or ignoring our difficult parts. I write "without" doing those things, but the more accurate view would be to say that we actually *can't* get to authentic, thoroughgoing self-love as long as we're engaged in those forms of delusion or self-aggression. Common insights regarding the relationship we have with ourselves have been a great start, but we need to go deeper if we're going to truly uncover the energy of love and then direct it inward to the parts of us that we have habitually deemed unlovable.

SENDING AND RECEIVING LOVE WITHIN

Bruce soon shared with me that the physical assault he suffered in college was not his first time feeling helpless in the midst of active abuse. He had grown up with an alcoholic father who verbally assaulted him, intimidated him, and routinely disappeared. His mother, though well-meaning, was also being abused and didn't have the wherewithal to adequately console Bruce, much less intervene on his behalf. Bruce was an only child from a working-class family, and he quickly learned that his safest bet was to shut down his needs for others and become incredibly self-reliant. This was a smart choice for a child to make in such an impossible and painful circumstance, but it created a paradigm for him in adulthood of constantly hiding from his own pain—until it literally barged into his bedroom.

In our sessions together, I supported Bruce in getting curious about his anxious parts and starting to ask them some of the questions put forth earlier in this book: "How long have you been protecting me in this way?" "Do you like being this way, or do you find it exhausting?" "If you could stop protecting me in this way and be another way, what would that look like?" These and other questions opened the doors for the anxious parts of him to conceive that another world might be possible. Next, we introduced to his defensive parts a new proposition: "If you allowed us to heal the parts inside that are holding the hurts from all these adverse experiences, maybe this world wouldn't feel like it's too much and too dangerous, and you wouldn't have to be so anxious anymore." This helped his defensive parts trust that the work we were doing had value. This was an important step, because we never want to do inner child work while our defenses are resisting it. Our defenses, after all, are the glue that has been holding our lives together this whole time. They truly deserve our respect and appreciation.

Over the course of a little more than a year, I helped Bruce to go inside, notice his wounded parts, unblend from them, and offer them the energy of caring and curiosity. He would go into memories, such as times he would be playing outside and his dad would periodically open the screen door to the house, shout nasty things at him, slam the screen door shut, and then return several minutes later to yell at him again. From a place of self-love, Bruce was able to converse with the part of him that was still carrying pain and vigilance from those experiences, bear witness to the story of what had happened, and, eventually, introduce that child part of him to some new perspectives: "Dad's no longer here. We're adults now, and we have this whole other life. We're much stronger now in so many ways. If we got hurt like that again, not only could we stand up for ourselves but we are also more resilient now and could find a way to be okay in the end. I'm Dad now."

There came a powerful session where Bruce went back into this memory to *reparent* that part. He helped his wounded inner child stand up to his father, to let him know that this was unacceptable and wrong. Bruce then brought that wounded part to live in a new place in his consciousness, a place that felt safe and connected to nature. He also offered that part of him a puppy to help his inner child feel protected.

Bruce later told me that the memory of what he experienced with his father wasn't the same after our session. We had effectively rewritten it. The emotional energy previously bound up in that memory was now gone. Was it just his imagination? You tell me. Because today, he's dating for the first time in seven years—and enjoying it. He has a job he likes, making more money than he's ever made before. He has friends, takes risks, and lets himself be seen. And the anxiety is gone. The sharp edge of electric fear and urgency forever in the background of his experience: gone. "I actually thought that's just how life felt," he said one session.

"It's almost weird that it's not there anymore." Here's my favorite part: he's gone back to school—to become a therapist, in fact. Having healed himself, Bruce's life is now centered on the question, "What can I give back? How can I be a vessel for the same transformation in others?"

∧ ∧ ∧

In the rest of part 2 of this book, we'll explore the tenderness that we can discover and encourage using the kind of process paradigm demonstrated in the above case study with Bruce. This approach is fundamentally based on a pluralistic view of the self. So much of what the self-love movement gets wrong is the result of viewing the self as some kind of monolithic and singular entity. That's how we've been taught to experience ourselves. But when we put ourselves under the microscope, when we take a good look inside, that view starts to unravel. We begin to experience our inner lives as fluid, dynamic, multifaceted, vast, and surprising.

Acknowledging the plurality of our being brings the concept of self-love into cogency. For to be self-loving at the level of feeling and inner relationship necessarily entails being both the sender and receiver of love. If we are of the mindset that we are a solid, unitary self, then how on earth would the sending and receiving of self-love take place? Who sends and who receives? Similarly, who is the inner critic and who is the one being criticized? Where does this leave us in the moment when feelings of being unlovable arise—not to mention feelings of outright self-loathing? Such a view leaves us stranded on an island of negative self-regard, with no paddleboat.

Thankfully, we contain multitudes. Thankfully, it is possible to notice when, for example, our inner critic has taken over, unblend from that part of us, locate the more generous and empathetic energy within us, and engage in a more elevated dialogue with the inner critic from there. This is a model of self-love that doesn't ask for us to contort ourselves in any way.

This framework offers us a model of self-love that has room for the difficult social realities that many of us face but are often left out of the conversation. Self-love must mean love of the whole self. This requires taking into account the social narratives about aspects of ourselves—our race, gender, sexual orientation, body type, and so forth—that condition our inner worlds and are among the primary reasons why many of our wounded, defensive, or angry parts came to have such prominent roles in our lives in the first place. To talk about self-love without mentioning the social structures and conditions that we face is to leave out a critical part of the picture.

There is a plurality to our being: We are one heart with many parts. We are one psyche holding many minds and many psychologies. This opens doors, and they are doors that urgently need opening, because, like Bruce, while we are not responsible for the conditioning that's brought us where we are now, we are indeed accountable for what we do with it.

5 I CAN'T EVEN

When You Feel Like You've Got Nothing Left to Give

Pain is important: how we evade it,
how we succumb to it, how we deal with it,
how we transcend it.
—*Audre Lorde*

» **THE** night before I checked into rehab found me resorting to childish tactics. On the floor, wailing like a character in a Greek tragedy, begging my girlfriend to let me stay. But I couldn't stay. I had stolen from her, been untrue, relapsed a dozen times, and, frankly, my life was in danger. It was rehab or the street: that was her tough-love ultimatum. But I was terrified of the uncertainty I was about to step into. I was terrified I'd fail. Cocaine and heroin had become my entire world, a cozy hell, and I was certain I didn't have what it took to climb out of the hole I had dug for myself. I was also certain I had to at least try.

The next day, I walked into rehab and immediately took a seat next to the front door, hoping no one would notice me. A man walked up to me and smiled: "Don't you worry, whiteboy. You're gonna be just fine." I later learned about this man's previous career robbing people at gunpoint in hotel elevators. More importantly, I came to know the decent person underneath all that. He had simply known a deeper desperation than I did because his trauma was just that severe. It was the same with everyone in there: whether they had been sex workers, pimps, thieves, gangbangers, tweakers, needle junkies, crack smokers, drunks . . . we were all utterly human, had been wrung through the wringer of life, and spit out on this side of things. Addiction is the derivative of trauma and tragedy. Every time. I came to know and love the humanity I saw in each one of us. I was transformed by it. I then took advantage of the opportunity to engage in intensive therapy, to throw myself deeply into meditation, and to do the work to heal.

Sorting out my life seemed impossible. I was certain I didn't have what it took, and it was all excruciating at first. Yet, none of those things mattered in the end. I found a way to stay in the game.

But life wasn't done teaching me this lesson that it tries fervently to teach us all. Out of rehab, I felt a deep calling to become a psychotherapist, meditation teacher, and yoga instructor—to find a way to integrate these things that had been given to me and offer them back to the world. This meant starting community college at the age of thirty with no money, no help from family, 100 percent on student loans, while still very much dealing with an active depression and trauma-related dysfunctional behavior patterns. One part of me knew I could pull it off. That part of me told me that we'd just take it one thing at a time, one day at a time. Just like rehab, it'd be hard, it'd seem like forever, we'd get through it, and it'd be worth it in the end. Other parts of me screamed loudly that the endeavor was impossible—it was too big, too audacious, and there were too many obstacles. One part liked to add that I was a junkie loser who'd never accomplished anything. But then I'd come back to the part of me that said, "Just do the next thing. All you have to do now is whatever's right in front of you." It was the quieter of the two voices, and I often had to go looking for it, but I learned I could rely on that voice. How curious that the *more tender voice* was the one that helped me to persist through difficulty. Rather than the harshness of self-aggression, ambition, and "powering through"—the voice that had always led me straight back to the needle—the voice of tenderness suggested that I really could do what I wanted to do, and that the way to do it was one step at a time.

Perhaps the most valuable thing I learned in school came from the way these themes repeated each and every finals season. Twice a year for six years, I'd be sitting with a pile of work that felt insurmountable. It seemed like I'd literally have to find a way to bend space-time in order to accomplish it all. I'd look at my classmates who had money from their parents, who were younger and more resilient than me, who didn't hold a lifetime of hurt and addiction in their bones— they all seemed so cut out for this, but not me. Certainly not me. But then that other voice in me would chime in, "All you have to do is write the next sentence. Read the next page. Breathe through one more hour. Smoke a damn cigarette if you must. But just keep going. It will end. And when it ends you will have proved something to yourself."

The essence of these stories is not unique to me. Anytime life backs us into a corner and we choose rising over recoiling, we are met with voices that scream, "I can't even! I don't have what it takes. That's for other people who have it better. It feels impossible. It's too painful, too much sacrifice. I'm gonna blow it and I'm not sure I can face that." But we all simultaneously hear a whisper, a quieter and calmer voice that says something akin to "Oh, but you can. You just need to find a way to take the next step. And then the one after that. It's just time to get resourceful. It's just time to summon your resilience. That's all."

The voice we heed is the voice that will get stronger.

GIVE UP OR GET UP

What convincingly feels impossible is often utterly possible. It simply entails failure and the kind of tenacity required to transcend failure. The idea of failure is agonizing for many of us. Failure convincingly feels like a confirmation that we are no good, undeserving, outcasts. Those voices are parts of us that either want to see us do better or are so freaked out by the vulnerability involved in going after our best lives that they're willing to assail us in an effort to keep us from trying. One option is to simply turn to those voices and say, "Thanks so much for taking care of me." Despite obvious appearances, that's what those voices are actually trying to do.

Notice that I'm lifting up a different model of tenacity here. Not the self-negating, hypermasculine, "no pain no gain" kind of stick-to-itiveness so often preached in our society. That kind of tenacity often entails shoving our feelings aside, which is dehumanizing and objectifying. I'm talking about a more tender kind of tenacity that is, in so many ways, the stronger and more courageous choice. It's the choice to allow our fears and freak-outs to be present so that we can relate to them. In situations where we are working at the very edge of what we think is possible, we can show these parts something incredibly valuable: that it's okay to be afraid, it's okay to fail, it's okay if it hurts, it's okay if we are humbled by it all. It's okay because we bounce back, we're resilient. We are built for such things.

So often, the feeling of failure is the sensation of growth. Seeing this is an invitation to reframe our relationship to failure. Personally, I've come to aim for failure. Failure, I've found, is actually the fastest path to self-actualization. This doesn't mean we try to fail or quit early. It means we aim to meet and stretch our limits as far as we can. If we aim for that mark, we will always be doing our best, we will always be working on excellence, and we will reach our goal every time—because our goal was to fail. You can feel successful every time that you reach that natural failure point.

You don't have to believe in yourself. You don't have to think positively. You don't have to wait until you're no longer afraid or in pain to make a move—and you don't have to shut down the pain and the fear in order to make a move, either. These common tropes aren't part of my story, and they don't have to be part of yours. You can absolutely not believe in yourself, be afraid, be in pain, hate it all, and still take the next step anyhow. You can hear all of those screams of "No!" and still follow the tender whisper of "Yes."

Personally, I'm working on becoming good friends with pain and fear. For if pain and fear were no longer a problem, what problems would I have left? If one is friends with pain and fear, one is free.*

KEY FACTORS OF RESILIENCE

Being able to bounce back and keep going even when it feels like we've got nothing left isn't just a matter of choice, though. Listening to that quiet inner voice that wants to set our direction in life is a great skill, a crucial one. And, the

---

* For the record, I mean "free" like the way Malcolm X talked about becoming free while still in prison: mentally, emotionally, spiritually free.

research is clear that there are conditions we can call into our lives that bolster the inner resources that foster good, continual bounce-backs.

- » **Community.** Show me who you hang with and I'll show you who you are.
- » **Identity.** Where your head goes, the rest of you follows.
- » **Emotional literacy.** Recognize what you're feeling when you feel it. Put language around it.
- » **Emotional intelligence.** Pause. Unblend. Get curious. Open the doorway to new choices.
- » **Self-talk.** Speak to yourself only as you would to another person—another person who deserves a baseline of respect and mercy.
- » **Spirituality.** Develop a rich and meaningful inner life. Connect to what matters daily.
- » **Make meaning of your experience.** Look for the lessons. Let crisis push you to dig deeper and get stronger. Let your challenges inspire you to help others.
- » **Resourcefulness.** Hard times are a call to get beyond-the-box creative. See the practice "Summoning Inner Resources" on page 97 to help get you there.

Of course, social and material privilege are among the biggest predictors of resilience as well, but they are far from the only ones.

We all hurt and we all heal. It is what we were born to do. Resilience is intrinsic to all living organisms. We can look to the experience of physical exercise as a direct corollary. We exercise with the intention of getting stronger and more flexible, but exercise doesn't do either of those things—not directly. Working out actually injures you. It creates tiny tears in your muscles. We strengthen in the rest and recovery *after* the workout. Thus, the intention behind a really good workout is to injure you manageably, just enough so that you'll emerge from your recovery stronger and more flexible than you were before. Same with life. Same with our hearts. Except we don't need to go looking for emotional workouts. They arrive at our doorstep without us even asking. We have endless opportunities to get bruised by life and then to strengthen in our recovery from it all. And from that kind of activity comes something most precious: confidence. As we repeatedly witness ourselves getting hurt and dealing with it skillfully—and thus consistently find ourselves stronger and more emotionally agile than before—our fear of life decreases. Our defensive parts start to get the message that we are stronger and more capable than we were in childhood—which is when our core defenses were conditioned and wired into us. We become indefatigable. Ever more courageous. Outrageously courageous, even. And this is but a glimpse of what's possible for us all.

Cultivating the factors of resilience I've listed above so very often boils down to the things we're saying yes to. Who we're in community with is up to us. How we speak to ourselves is often on autopilot—but we can choose to get off autopilot and harness the inner conversation. Cultivating an inner life, perhaps through things like meditation, contemplation, study, and therapy, may mean changing some of our habits and routines to make space for deeper things. In order to say yes to deepening our resources and quickening our capacity for bounce-back, we might need to do something that freaks many of us out more than failure does—say no.

6

THE BEAR WE MUST LEARN TO BEAR

The Guilt of Saying No

> "No" is golden. "No" is the kind of power the good witch wields. It's the way whole, healthy, emotionally evolved people manage to have relationships with jackasses while limiting the amount of jackass in their lives.
>
> —*Cheryl Strayed*

» **ENTIRE** precious lives have gone half-lived behind the thought, "But I don't want to upset anybody." Almost every well-intentioned person I know has difficulty discerning the line between this form of codependence and compassion. The list that follows is simple and even reductive but also a game-changing reminder. It is also not a moral code, and these are not maxims that are always a good idea. In fact, if you followed this list to a tee, it could be a recipe for being a terrible person. But that doesn't erase the following truths:

- » You are allowed to say no.
- » You are allowed to not be nice about it.
- » You are allowed to not offer any explanations as to why.

» You are allowed to not know why you are saying no.

» You are allowed to not care at all what the other person feels as a result.

» You are allowed to care about what the other person feels without taking their feelings to be your own.

» You are allowed to care about what the other person feels—and nonetheless not display to them that you care how they feel, in order to avoid getting tangled back up with that person.

» You are allowed to take measures to avoid getting tangled back up with someone after you've set a boundary.

» You are allowed to discern whose emotions are whose in a situation and only tend to your own.

» You are allowed to not make sense to anyone else.

» You are allowed to walk away at any time.

As you read that, a barrage of *but!* and *what if!* and *I'm not ready!* may have bubbled up inside you. This list is completely and utterly independent of that. None of those "buts" coming from your defensive parts erase these simple truths. Check to see if you find guilt or fear embedded in any reactions you had to reading that. You likely have something to get curious about and process here. I invite you to consider working with that fear and guilt. Working with fear and guilt is often just the price of admission to realms of personal liberation.

THE COMPASSIONATE NO

Think about the last time you said yes to something when inside of you there was really a no. Something was asked of you, perhaps to show up some place or to do something for someone, and you said yes when, *in your body*, there was a sensation of no. It might have seemed selfish to say no. You might have such a strong habit of giving in to others, or perhaps have even come to enjoy letting others set the agenda, that you didn't even "hear" or "feel" the no—and yet it was there, somehow. Indeed, most of us who don't have the greatest feel for our boundaries often don't realize that there was a no there until after the fact. After we've gotten home from the draining event, after we're already entangled in some half-hearted commitment, after a toxic person who drains us is walking all over us yet again—*then* we realize we made the wrong choice: that we should've spoken up for ourselves.

To be clear, there are situations in which we feel resistance to things that are good for us, like meditation, exercise, or spending time with someone who challenges us in healthy ways. That's not the kind of no I'm talking about. That's the kind of no we'd do well to get curious about, or maybe learn how to gently dance past so we can move closer to our truest desires. That kind of no is a selfish no. Being able to decipher between a *selfish* no and a *compassionate* no is part of what this chapter is about.

A compassionate no is the kind you feel when you're asked to go to an event and you are tapped out. Or when you find yourself planning a trip to see someone, possibly a family member, who's frequently abusive toward you. Or when you're in the presence of someone who has drained your energy so many times in the past and here you are, feeling that sense of depletion, while fake-smiling and trying to cover up how badly you want to head for the hills. That's the kind of no we need to heed more often in the process of reparenting ourselves.

THE BODY IS OUR COMPASS

Stop and remember a time like one of those no's I just described. Take a breath, slow down, and really relive the experience in your mind's eye. What happened? How did you feel? What thoughts went through your mind? What did your body feel like? Do that, take some mental notes, and then come back.

Most importantly: What happened in your body? Was there a tightness somewhere? Where was it? Was there a heaviness? An anxiety? What happened in your shoulders? In your belly? In your arms and legs? Beyond the body, can you recognize this event in general as being a pattern in your life? Maybe a pattern with this particular person or with a sort of situation that keeps repeating itself?

The bodily guidance system I'm pointing toward with these questions is that of our *soma* (Greek for "living body"), which is constantly talking to us, sending us signals and information. The problem is that the true, intuitive voice of the soma is often crowded out by too many competing inner voices. If we practice sensitizing ourselves to our bodies, such as with the "Grounding: Body of Breath" practice on page 94, that sense will become clearer. If we actually listen for and follow through with the guidance we're receiving, that sense will become clearer still. And if we do the work of healing the trauma almost all of us hold in our bodies, that voice will begin to get loud and clear as a bell.

It's important to think of checking in with your bodily felt sense as a practice, because there's plenty of momentum in the habit of saying yes. When it comes to saying no and holding boundaries, the fear of feeling guilty is perhaps the number one overriding force of our sense of no. We don't want to let anyone down. We fear what they might think of us.

We fear the backlash. We fear what might happen to someone if we don't show up or help in some way. We see someone with a need we technically could help them address, and so we feel it's our responsibility. We feel obligated. All of this means that there's a certain tenderness we have to cultivate in saying "no." We can learn to acknowledge that we truly *want* to be helpful people, responsive people, and that doing so involves saying "no" much more than we thought it did.

In countless sessions, clients have told me about painfully tangled interpersonal webs they find themselves in. I typically ask, "Why didn't you say no?" only to have the response come back, "I would've felt guilty." My follow-up question: "Which is worse, the situation you're in now or the guilt you would have felt?" Which one is more intense? Which one lasts longer? Guilt is indeed a bear of an emotion: a formidable beast we dread meeting with in the vast forest of life, but we must learn to hold it. We must learn to bear the bear of guilt if we want to stay true to ourselves and not cause harm with our codependency, however subtle. Holding space for the bear of guilt is often one of the kindest things we can do—for ourselves, for those with whom we're in codependent relationships, and as an example to others.

That's step one: to be willing to feel the guilt in the wake of saying no or holding some sort of boundary. Step two would be to acknowledge the toxic shame embedded in the guilt and to offer the energy of curiosity or self-love to that part of you, such as with the practices on pages 53–56.

DUCK BREAD

There's one last consequence that I'd like to discuss about saying yes even when you feel a no in your body. It's the most common one: resentment.

Marshall Rosenberg, author of *Nonviolent Communication*, discusses the concept of *memnoon*, an Arabic word that roughly translates to "the request that blesses the giver." Rosenberg translates this as, "Please do as I request *only* if you can do so with the joy of a little child feeding bread to a hungry duck. Please do not do as I request if there is any taint of fear of punishment . . . [or] you would feel guilty if you don't."[4] A client of mine once abbreviated this to "duck bread" so that it'd be easier to remember. Basically, if we're not feeling a full yes about something, it might be best to say no and to bear whatever comes up as a result. After all, would you want somebody showing up for *you* begrudgingly? Or only because they feel obligated to? Or, worse yet, only because they fear being on the receiving end of you shaming them if they don't?

When interactions are imbalanced in this manner, an iota of resentment is generated and stored away. Over time, with repeated experiences such as this, those iotas really begin to add up. Resentment is one of the greatest usurpers of love and affection on the planet. I can't tell you how many couples have landed on my therapy couch full of stored resentments that have slowly eaten away at what was once a beautiful and nourishing connection. I find consistently in such situations that one or both of them have long been tolerating and bottling things they should have refused at the onset. But they didn't. What could have been a simple, "Hey, that doesn't work for me, can we find another way?" years ago is now a seething heap of layered complexities of the kind that so often, and so heartbreakingly, never gets resolved.

^ ^ ^

Some friends of mine live in an intentional community in Brooklyn where they have a custom: when someone says no to something, to anything, the other person responds, "Thank you for taking care of yourself." This practice is borne of the awareness that if you don't take care of you, I'll end up having to do that in some way down the line. If your plate is already too full and you don't express your no to my birthday party or performance or brunch invitation—if you say yes instead—I might get my way, but the price tag of resentment in our relationship is just too expensive.

"No" is often the most compassionate option on the table. But, as mentioned above, it will be difficult to connect with that soft, inner voice that says "no" if we're strongly habituated to saying "yes." This practice—and in truth, all of the parts work practices in this book—becomes so much easier when we devote some time to practices of embodiment that help us sense ourselves with greater refinement. With that in mind, let's talk about meditation.

7

ABOUT THAT MEDITATION PRACTICE YOU'RE KINDA SORTA SOMETIMES MAYBE DOING

The fruitfulness of our lives depends in large measure on our ability to doubt our own words and to question the value of our own work. The [hu]man who completely trusts [their] own estimate of [them]self is doomed to sterility.
—*Thomas Merton*

» I attempted what I thought was meditation for the first time when I was nineteen. I was a straight up spare-change-begging crust-punk kid who could've cared less about meditation—but I'd fallen in love. In fact, I had become hopelessly, over-the-moon-infatuated with a drum-circle-loving, patchouli-drenched hippie. We worked together at a juice bar where I'd overheard her telling a coworker she wished she meditated "but just couldn't find the time." (Sound familiar?) I thought she might eventually ask me if I had ever tried it, and I knew I'd score major points if I was able to say that I had. So, I did what I was sure all adept meditators do: I rolled an enormous joint and smoked until I couldn't remember my last name. I then sat painfully cross-legged on my patio and visualized words like "peace," "love," and "light" floating toward me in big, psychedelic, '70s bubble letters. After about ninety seconds of this I figured I had done enough research to speak with authority about the practice, and I called it a day. And it worked! A couple days later, my work-crush asked me if I knew anything about meditation, and I had a bona fide experience under my belt to tell her about. "It feels so good to go so deep," I reported. It wasn't a lie so much as it was completely untrue. But, hey, anything for love.

BEYOND THE HAZE OF ASSUMPTION

Okay, this one's more fictional. Except for the part where it describes something that we all do, me included.

Once upon a time, an aspiring student asked a Zen master to teach them meditation. The master agreed to teach the student but requested that they first tell the master all that they knew about meditation. The student proceeded to go on a long tirade about fanciful things they had read in spiritual books and speculative ideas about what meditation would do for them and the cool things their friends were saying about it all. While the student talked and talked the master handed them a cup and began pouring tea. The student's cup became full, but the master didn't stop. The tea began overflowing and spilling everywhere. The student shrieked at the master: "It's full! *Why are you still pouring*?" The master smiled: "Oh? You mean I shouldn't try to add anything to a cup that's already full?"

There is little we can learn if we step toward something feeling sure that we already "get it." There's no room for fresh, life-altering insight if we're already full of preconceived notions. The student's allegorical "cup" was already so full of presumptions about meditation that the master saw that more instructions wouldn't have been of any real use to the student. That is, when we empty ourselves of what we think meditation is and how it should go, we make space for the real practice to begin.

But a full cup isn't the only mindset we'd be wise to check ourselves for if we are endeavoring for the inner revolution meditation holds for us. We could also have a "dirty" cup, meaning that our intentions aren't so pure. There are those among us who would try meditation just to impress their work-crush, after all. There's a more subtle game we sometimes play, too. When I was training as a therapist, a mentor of mine warned me to be on the lookout for clients who come to therapy in order to bolster a self-story of "I'm getting my shit together; I went to therapy today!" but then wouldn't do the work in between sessions and weren't sincere about making a change. She warned me of this not out of judgment but because I would be doing such a person a grave disservice should I not bring it to their attention. A person could stay in such a self-delusion their entire lives, really, and never see it. We are all susceptible to this. It's a subtle form of self-hatred, and it's heartbreaking.

We could also have a cup with a big hole in it, meaning we dismiss the potential depth of the practice (perhaps by meditating while stoned off our rocker) and the instructions and rich insights embedded in the practice go "in one ear and out the other."

^ ^ ^

Meditation indeed seems to be one of those things that people feel like they've got more or less dialed-in after five months but after fifteen years come to the realization that they know almost nothing about it. Most of what we call "meditation" today consists of vast and subtle practices with a lot of layers to them that almost no one fully understands. Whatever our practice is—be it silent sitting or mantra or chakras or Reiki or plant medicine—if we don't approach it honestly, earnestly, and with a willingness to humbly question ourselves, we're likely to be holding one of the aforementioned three cups.

A fourth kind of problematic cup would be one that doesn't have a lid, that allows anyone to pour tea in without questioning them. A healthy (but not overbearing) sense of skepticism is necessary in the spiritual marketplace, an arena where shysters and snake oil salespeople have abounded for millennia. Perhaps the most common way we can get tricked is by trusting whatever "feels good" or "feels right." While I definitely advocate for people to develop and trust their intuitions in life, our ability to buy into cozy half-truths can't be ignored. Indeed, if we truly sense that such practices can take us to the brink of life-altering realization, why are we content to be less than thorough? I mean, you know what felt *so good* and *so spiritual* to me at one time? Heroin. You know what felt excruciatingly awful and wrong? Getting clean.

May we never forget: often the deepest truths are the ones that challenge us. May we develop the discernment to tell the difference. May we follow our gut in this practice, but may our brains follow closely behind.

IF IT CAN HEAL, IT CAN HURT: THE DANGERS OF MEDITATION

In the Chinese medical tradition, they have a saying: "If it can heal, it can hurt." After all, people leave yoga classes and go straight to the hospital every day. Hell, I once had a seizure doing intensive pranayama practices while several days into

a master cleanse. My hubris-ridden logic: "Heyyy, it's a healing practice—what could go wrong?" Healing practices are
like fire, though. They can bring a welcome warmth to what's
gone cold, and they can burn down the house. Their potency
is determined by the energy we bring to them. A case in point
is the tragedy of Megan Vogt, a woman who had a psychotic
break during a ten-day silent meditation retreat. No one at
the center knew how to deal with it both during and after the
retreat, and weeks later she committed suicide.[5]

Megan's awful story is an outlier, but at the very least it
must serve as a cautionary tale for the rest of us: meditation
practices can be powerful interventions into our mind and
body, and they can interact with trauma or incipient psycho-
sis in ways we should know about.[6] Did the meditation *cause*
her psychotic break? Not likely. Did the meditation create the
conditions for her break to manifest? Most certainly.

Even if you're not someone who's suffered a lot of trauma
or who's currently dealing with mental illness, there's an immediate danger we all face with any contemplative or healing
practice: such practices can be used to reinforce subtle forms
of self-division and even self-hatred. We can utilize various
defensive parts of ourselves to shield us from the inherent
vulnerability of the practice. Our perfectionist parts might
come in and enforce a habitual rigidity. Our dissociative
parts might show up and have us zone out for eleven out of
ten minutes. Our inner critic might run wild telling us we're
doing it all wrong, we never get anything right. The parts
of us that long for a silver bullet, for some sort of salvation,
might convince us that we've finally found the panacea we've
been looking for, and now we just need to get *real devotional*
about all this, and we'll finally be cured.

Perhaps the most widespread danger of all: we could go
on a mission to rid ourselves of "ego." When we talk about

our ego as something bad, it's just self-hatred wearing a spiritual disguise. In the Eastern traditions, what's referred to as "ego" is shorthand for a cluster of defensive parts of us that don masks of self-centeredness, avoidance, and pettiness to circumvent perceived vulnerability. Consider, though, that "defense mechanism" literally means "something in me that's trying to keep me *safe*." Therefore, the big, nasty "ego" that's been slandered in most if not all spiritual traditions is actually just our inner defenders doing what they think will help us. These are parts of us that are well-intentioned, no matter what the surface-level appearance. Yes, they are parts of us that need to evolve and change, but hatred and judgment rarely help anyone grow. Only love can do that.

What's more, these are parts of us that aren't going anywhere. You can't lop off a part of your own psyche—and some of the scandals involving leaders of spiritual communities are directly linked to the delusion that one can. The so-called ego is a roommate that we can't get rid of, so it certainly makes sense to establish kindly and reliable channels of communication with it.

It's the function of meditation to help us notice such inner dynamics. They are examples of the practice acting as a nice, clean mirror in which we can see the result of our deep conditioning. Seeing more clearly, we can pause, unblend, and get curious about the drama unfolding before our closed eyes. If we can put some daylight between us and our mental-emotional experience, we will have the opportunity to befriend each of these parts of us and harmonize our lives from the inside out. False identities, or defenses that are simply no longer useful, will then drop away naturally. The problem is, we so often don't take that wakeful step back; we remain blended with the parts of us trying to "do meditation" when meditation is, necessarily, an undoing.

GREEN LIGHTS ON THE ENLIGHTENMENT HIGHWAY

Having leveled all these critiques at meditation-gone-wrong, perhaps we can pause and unblend right now. Because it's not all so serious. In a certain light, it is hilarious what we do to ourselves, these unnecessary struggles we put ourselves through in the name of well-being. Meditation itself, seen at this angle, is itself a little bit ridiculous. The next time you're practicing in a group setting, take a look around you. Yes, it's beautiful to see fellow humans engaging in earnest efforts to get free. It's also absurd that we should work so hard when all we're actually trying to do is drop our masks and become who we truly are. If we lose levity as a result of this practice, something is definitely amiss.

My first teacher, Amma, once told a story about a man who came to her after having experiences both wonderful and strange in meditation. He was seeing all kinds of flashing green lights while he chanted his mantra, and he wondered what they meant. Was he entering other dimensions? Was he reaching some new advanced stage of practice? Was he becoming enlightened?! What did it mean?! "It means you shouldn't drive for a while," Amma told him. The man was perplexed. "One of your green flashing lights might appear when you come to a red light. I'm afraid you might drive into the intersection and hurt somebody!"

Amma was, in her typical childlike way, lifting up the truth that experiences such as these—up to and including authentically mystical ones—aren't the point in meditation. The point is to apply ourselves earnestly and to keep being curious about whatever it is we meet in the practice. The point is to uncover the heart's natural qualities of love, compassion, appreciation, and resilience—and to extend those qualities to the neurotic, afflicted, and conflicted parts of our inner family. The point is what develops over time in our day-to-day lives, not so much what goes down in our individual sessions on the cushion. The Buddhist nun Tenzin Palmo once commented that the people best able to tell us if we're advancing in our meditation are those in our families (biological or chosen). Do the people who are sometimes the most difficult to be around think that we're becoming kinder? That's the real litmus test.

^ ^ ^

To conclude this chapter on meditation, my question to you is this: When was the last time you consciously took a breath? Do you know how to take a proper, full, satisfying breath? And now that you're breathing deeply because you feel like I caught you in the act—*you bad, shallow breather, you!*—does it make sense for me to say: What are we even doing trying to "follow the breath" when we don't really know *how* to breathe? How can we expect to reach for the heavens when we don't know how to walk on the earth? Even if a person's practice is mantra or Reiki or something else, I'm not sure *any* practice is going to have much of an impact on someone if they average one deep breath every three days (or years), or if their body is bound up with tension from overworking, trauma, and poor lifestyle choices.

And no practice is going to shift our life if we don't know how to simply hang out with ourselves, just as we are, with no modifications required. Without that kind of self-acceptance, dare I say self-love, as a baseline, any practice risks turning into a contest between our "good meditator" part and our "bad self" part. We are not here to "kill our ego," or to get rid of any part of ourselves. If we stand in judgment—shaming the thinking mind, hating our self-centeredness, referring to any part of ourselves with any recrimination whatsoever—it is full-stop, out-and-out self-abuse.

Thus, as you visit the following practice, "Grounding: Body of Breath," I invite you to set aside whatever you've heard about mindfulness and TM and crystals and chakras, the whole lot of it. Including the idea that your thoughts aren't allowed here. Or that distractions can't coexist with you hanging out with yourself. Let's just take a step back from all the fanciful things we think we know and figure out how to enjoy the most basic, fundamental, human thing: a functional breath.

I, your meditation teacher, officially give you permission to not meditate, to just let your thoughts and emotions run free like the wild horses that they are, and to let whatever's happening in your environment just go on. Give up. Surrender the self-improvement project. You're not a fixer-upper. I invite you to nourish your nervous system at the cellular level and simply be curious about wherever that takes you instead.

PART TWO PRACTICES

» Grounding: Body of Breath

In this practice exercise, you'll be learning how to do the single most nourishing physical behavior a person can do.

First, if you aim to take in a full breath, you'll need to arrange your body in such a way that your airflow isn't obstructed. You can accomplish this by either sitting up straight or by lying down on your back. If you go the lying-down route, I suggest placing something under your knees, such as a couple of pillows, so you don't hurt your back. But no pillows under your head, please. That would put your neck out of alignment and obstruct airflow. Instead, try using a towel folded so that it only lifts your head about an inch off the ground. You can do this in bed if you must, but lying on a rug or yoga mat on the ground is going to be much better for your skeletal alignment. If you're sitting up straight, try to be neither rigid nor lax about it.

Either way, determine how long you will practice for (ten minutes is great if you're new to this sort of thing; twenty minutes is great if it ain't your first trip to the rodeo) and set a timer on your phone or another device. Commit to staying in the game until the timer goes off. Being disciplined about this one rule will serve you very well in the long run.

Start by noticing what it's like to be in your body. Notice that it's a breathing body. Begin taking full breaths into the lower belly. It might be easiest to get a full breath if you breathe through the mouth for both inhale and exhale, at least at first. Breathe into the lowest part of the belly, beneath the navel, what's called the *dantien* in the Chinese system. Breathe in and feel the belly expand in all directions out in front of you. Breathe out and feel the belly simply collapse as you do so. What's actually causing your belly to expand like this is your diaphragm—a dome-shaped muscle that sits just below the bottom tip of your breastbone. You can imagine it flattening downward as you breathe in and rising back into its dome shape as you breathe out.

Try to achieve close to full inhalations and exhalations, but please don't be forceful. You're doing this in order to nourish yourself and wake up the body, so let your attitude reflect that. Keep breathing. This may feel like a bit of work at first, and there's always the temptation to bail out, but just look past that and keep going. This is going to produce a desirable effect, a bit of a natural high, by the end, so let the benefit be your motivation to simply keep going. As you feel the belly begin to loosen up and soften a bit, you can make the breath deeper, slower, and longer. See how quiet you can make the breath as well—but, again, no need to be a perfectionist about any of this. There's no pressure here. Just a body breathing in and out of the low belly.

Notice that when you breathe in, the top parts of your hips roll forward a little and aid in you taking a full breath. As you breathe out, the hips slide backward a little and aid in the exhalation. You can go with that and allow your hips to roll forward and backward in a slightly more pronounced way to deepen this. Keep breathing.

I've got to acknowledge that breathing and expanding the belly can be psychologically uncomfortable for many of us, especially women who've internalized messages from our culture regarding what shape our belly ought to be. If that speaks to you, please consider this belly breathing to be a giant, compassionate, self-affirming, self-loving, rebellious middle finger to all that dehumanizing conditioning. We love big bellies in this practice. Big, full, round, third-trimester-style bellies are to be celebrated in the space of this practice. If you're stuck in shame about that, please be kind to the ashamed part of you. Tell them it's okay and safe to do this. You might even imagine our culture's ridiculous standards as a giant hand that's gripped around you, suffocating you. With each breath you take, you're prying those fingers off you, one at a time, little by little.

Once you feel you've established good, deep breathing in the belly, begin allowing the breath to continue upward into the chest. The belly fills up and expands omnidirectionally—in front, to the sides, and you can even imagine a bit of space filling out around the back—then it moves up into the chest where it causes the ribs to expand out to the left and the right. As the chest expands, you'll feel your ribs spreading out away from one another like an accordion. As you breathe out, allow the chest to simply melt and then the belly the same. In other words, breathing in we go from the bottom up; breathing out we go from the top down; and we keep an eye on abstaining from rigidity or tensing up the whole time.

Slow, long, deep, full, easy, and silent.

This ought to begin to feel nourishing and satisfying at some point. You're bringing new life to your cells—knocking rust off the pipes, so to speak. You're detoxing your organs and stretching your lungs. You're sending good fuel to the brain. You're also building muscle. There are three main groups of muscles involved in the act of breathing, and due to our pervasive tendency to "forget to breathe," these muscles wither. As you build them back up, you'll naturally begin breathing more deeply throughout the day. You'll also remember to take conscious breaths more often. It's possible to reach the point when even a single conscious breath is enough to reconnect with your inner world and remind you of your deeper intentions.

Keep enjoying this simple process until your timer goes off.

» Summoning Inner Resources

What follows is a visualization practice designed to put you in touch with your own inner resources. Sometimes when it seems like we are at an impasse, we're not—we actually just (as the Beatles put it) need a little help from our friends. This practice utilizes our capacity for imagination as a doorway to the unconscious mind, a place where we can find just that. I would consider this practice to be "parts work adjacent"— another way of getting at the same inner territory. Also, if you've been struggling with getting to the energy of curiosity or caring for your parts, this practice very well may help you to begin recognizing this presence within you.

Sit comfortably. Take a few deep breaths and settle into being here with yourself. Then, think of a difficult situation—either something you're dealing with right now or something that's coming your way in the future. It could be large or small. It could be at work, at home, with a friend or family member, a financial situation—anything.

Once you have the situation you want to work with, imagine you're faced with it in this very moment. Play the movie of it in your mind's eye. See the situation unfolding, notice your feelings, how your body feels in the situation, and how you're inclined to act. Notice also who else is present, what their presence feels like, what their voice sounds like; imagine as many aspects of the situation as you can.

Suddenly, time freezes and everything stops. Out of the thin air, a luminous being begins to materialize, little by little. It's someone you know to be possessed of great wisdom and insight, someone you admire, someone loving and courageous and strong. It could the Buddha or Maya Angelou or David

Bowie or your grandmother or someone else. Watch as the being slowly manifests before you. Who is it?

What do they look like? See their face, their eyes, their smile; feel their presence, the warmth of their gaze. Looking upon them, you tell them about the situation you're facing, and you ask if they might help you. "Of course," they say. "I would love nothing more." The luminous being says, "Here, let me show you how I would handle this," and, much to your surprise, they step right into your body and take over. You're still there, but it's like you're in the backseat and they've taken the steering wheel. What does it feel like to have them in your body? What do you notice about how your vibe is shifting, how your facial expression is changing, even the tone of your voice?

Time starts back up. You watch as the luminous being handles the situation, sees to all concerns, and communicates with everyone involved. What's it like? What do they say? What do they do? How do they carry themselves and speak? What sort of emotional qualities do they exhibit? What sort of empathy do they display, and how do they communicate their needs, wants, and boundaries? How do others respond to them? Take your time and watch them handle everything with all the grace and intelligence they possess.

With your affairs sufficiently handled (or at least as handled as they're going to get today), the being steps back out of your body. You're so grateful to them. The being then tells you they have some special words of advice for you. They bend down, draw their face close to your ear, and whisper words of wisdom. What do they say?

Finally, they hold out their hands, and you see that they're holding a bright, shimmering box made of gold and silver. They tell you that they want for you to never forget what's transpired here today. They especially don't want you to forget your own strength and wisdom. In the box is a gift for you to remember all of this by. It's a powerful and meaningful symbol picked out just for you. You reach out and slowly open the lid of the box to find what's inside. What's there?

You take the symbolic object and cherish it for a moment. You share some parting words and gratitude with the luminous being. And, as you take a deep breath, they vanish back into thin air, the whole scene vanishes along with them, and you gently transition from the practice.

After the practice, take some time to write down everything you can remember about it, everything you saw, felt, and understood. Visualizations that evoke images and experiences from deeper layers of our consciousness are very much like dreams. If we engage with them, write them down, and maybe even talk about them, they'll stick to us in a meaningful way. If we don't engage with them and simply move on, they'll vanish into space, and it'll be just like they never happened. It's a fantastic idea to go out and acquire something resembling the gift that they gave you, too. It doesn't have to be the actual thing. It could be a picture of it—or even a picture you draw of it. Keep the object somewhere where you'll see it as a reminder of your own abundant resourcefulness, perhaps on your mirror or nightstand.

It might seem like this was all your imagination, but in a way, that's the point. Everything about the luminous being you imagined is already in you. You couldn't have imagined it otherwise.

» The Anxiety Interruption Tool Kit

Some bumper sticker wisdom: "If you're not freaking out, you're not paying attention." Anxiety is one of the most reasonable and appropriate responses to the condition of the world, and, simultaneously, we need you with both feet on the ground if we're to do anything about it.

I sat down with Nick Werber, an up-and-coming coach in Brooklyn whose family constellation workshops are gaining well-deserved traction, to discuss anxiety.[*] He offered some techniques from his grab bag of evidence-based modalities such as Integrative Hypnosis, Emotional Freedom Technique (EFT), and Somatic Experiencing (SE). You'll find four of these techniques below.

But before you dive into these short, practical exercises, please heed this important piece of advice: Don't mistake the beginning for the end. Say your anxiety is at a level eight or nine out of ten; these techniques can bring you down to a level five or six. Even so, they aren't intended to be a quick fix but rather a therapeutic tool for going deeper. In other words, if your anxiety is at a level eight, engaging in other processes for gathering insight and inspiration isn't really possible. In the four-step model I offered in chapter 3—pause, unblend, get curious, and shift your inner dialogue—these practices for addressing anxiety correspond to the "pause" step. With your anxiety down to a five or so, the subsequent steps become available. As Nick says, "For me it doesn't end with the interrupt. This is actually the beginning. Now that you're a bit more present, *now what?*"

THE SIDE-TO-SIDE INTERRUPT

1. Take an object into your right hand, any object that is big enough and light enough to hold in one hand—or simply imagine you're holding an object in your right hand.

---

[*] See https://nicknwerber.com.

2. Look straight ahead. Keep your gaze there the whole time, but no need to be too rigid about that.
3. With the object in your right hand and your arms relaxed so that the object is in the bottom of your peripheral vision, move your right hand as far as you can to the right while still being able to see it.
4. Bring your right hand back to center, pass the object to your left hand, and then move your left hand as far as you can while still being able to see it.
5. Bring your hand back to center, pass the object, and repeat.
6. Keep going for as long as needed.

THE PERIPHERAL VISION PATTERN INTERRUPT

1. Pick something to look at directly in front of you, such as any specific point on a wall.
2. Without moving your eyes, begin taking an inventory of everything you can see in your periphery. Notice what's on the left side of your peripheral field. Notice what's on the right. Notice what's up. And what's down. Notice what colors you can identify and mentally label—i.e., "blue," "green," and so on.
3. Keep going until your anxiety downshifts.
4. It can't hurt to breathe.

THE EFT TAPPING PATTERN INTERRUPT

1. Take your index and second finger and begin tapping gently, somewhat quickly (but not rushed or forceful), and rhythmically for five to twenty seconds in each of these places, one at a time and in order:

   » Third eye
   » Under one eye

- » Temple on same side
- » Upper lip below your nose
- » With an open palm on chest
- » Then, take one hand and wrap it around the opposite wrist while taking a deep breath in and out.

THE "VUU – AH" INTERRUPT

1. Take a deep breath into the belly.
2. As you exhale, say, "*Vuuuuuuu.*"
3. Take a deep breath.
4. As you exhale, say, "*Ahhhhhhh.*"
5. Repeat for two to three minutes.

» A New Depression Inventory Checklist: From One Depression Survivor to Another

If you're feeling like hell and your thoughts have taken a turn for the worst, before you collapse into despair let's check on a few things. First, I want to acknowledge that reading through this might feel pointless either now or as we progress. Let me suggest a metaphor that I find helpful.

Imagine for a moment that you're sitting in a movie theater and you see someone you know sitting three seats down from you. The movie hasn't started yet and you want to say hello to them. In order to do that, you're going to have to look past the three people sitting between you in order to look directly at the person you know and get their attention. You might even say, "Hey," while trying to project your voice past those three people so that your friend specifically hears you. I want you to do this with your emotions and thoughts as you sift through this. Your depression is the three people sitting between you and the person you want to say hi to. Look past these inner voices and focus on the questions and ideas here instead.

1. **Check to make sure you actually want to feel better.** Sometimes we think that we want to feel better, but we only *want to want* to feel better. We can be surprisingly invested in suffering sometimes. Our jadedness is ironic like that. So, get clear on the fact that you want to feel better. And, if you can't seem to, can you get curious about why not? Perhaps feeling like hell is benefiting you in a way that you haven't yet acknowledged to yourself. This was true for me at many points in my journey.

2. **Go outside.** If it seems like going outside would be too much for you to handle, consider that feeling to be a hypothesis. Go outside for five minutes and test your hypothesis and confirm if it's true or not. I've learned to never underestimate the power of a change of scenery, fresh air, and (especially) looking up at the sky.

3. **Operation: Hydration.** I sometimes wonder what my experience of childhood depression and trauma would have looked like if I had been even remotely hydrated at the time. Dehydration on its own can make you miserable—it can give you headaches, make you feel hopeless, make you feel lifeless and devoid of energy, make you feel irritable. I can remember times when the thought of drinking eight pint glasses (16 oz.) of water a day seemed like a great chore. But all you have to do is start with one glass right now. (And then keep going.)

4. **Remember fun?** Play is the opposite of anxiety. Play is the opposite of hopelessness. Adult play therapy is literally a thing.[7] Let yourself regress and do something you loved doing when you were a kid. Solo dance parties in the kitchen, epic air guitar performances in the mirror, and obnoxiously loud (and bad) sing-alongs are encouraged.

5. **Go green.** Real talk: choosing a salad over a sandwich can make the difference between a shitty day and a good one. I don't care if you have to smother it in ranch dressing, get some broccoli and lettuce in you.

6. **Breathe.** How can we feel better if we aren't tending to the root of our being? Your breath is among the most powerful tools you have at your disposal when it comes to your ability to influence your mental-emotional state.[8] The "Grounding: Body of Breath" practice on page 94 is good place to start. Give it ten minutes a day for several days before trying to gauge if it's working.

7. **Call a friend.** Cue the *Golden Girls* theme song. Getting your thoughts out of your head and into the world by saying them out loud (or even texting them) and having them received activates regions of your brain associated with emotional regulation and problem-solving. Don't feel like you have any friends or people you want to talk to? Here are some resources if you're in the United States:

   » The National Alliance on Mental Illness has a peer-led help line (meaning you'd talk to someone who's struggled with mental health issues also) you can reach 24/7 at 1-800-950-NAMI (6264).

   » NYC Well has a free talk or text message line that's 24/7 (it includes relay service for deaf and hard of hearing individuals as well as Spanish- and Mandarin- and Cantonese-speaking counselors) that you can access by texting "WELL" to 65173 or calling 1-888-692-9355.

   » The National Suicide Prevention Line is also available 24/7 at 1-800-273-8255.

» I have used these help lines myself. In the absence of someone you already know who gets you, they can be a surprisingly good substitute.

8. **Random Acts of Non-Cliché Kindness.** I say this without a shred of judgment or blame: a big part of depression is focusing on oneself. Our thoughts dwell on what's wrong with *us*, how awful it all feels to *us*, and how *our* problems can't be solved. You can disrupt that cycle by considering others. Lovingkindness meditation, for example, focuses on offering thoughts of well-being to others and has been shown to decrease depression and anxiety and increase feelings of amusement and life purpose. Volunteer gigs found on websites like idealist.org and volunteermatch.com are even better.

9. **Move.** What feels like the most impossible thing is often exactly what we need. This is true of exercise and depression. Just focus on getting dressed for exercise, whatever that might be. Getting to a class of some sort is ideal. I also love Coach Kozak's HASfit videos on YouTube because they're short and really positive. If you can't move your legs, there are cardio videos online that are done sitting down with just arm movements, and likewise there are videos with just leg movements. If you can move your body at all, you can get your heart rate up, sweat a little, and raise your serotonin level. Of course, you should check in with a doctor first and follow their recommendations.

A TIME TO UNDERSTAND

INTERLUDE

The Healing Power of Theory

» **SURVIVING** something difficult or traumatic and not knowing why the event happened can feel tremendously unsettling. Without a clear why, we can't string together a coherent narrative, and our nervous systems cannot rest. Our defensive parts are then left with a giant, gaping uncertainty that's endlessly frustrating to a brain whose job it is to make sense and meaning of things. In such situations, the brain tends to replay scenarios over and over again, constantly scanning for clues that'll help us fill in the blanks, trying to find the meaning of it all. When we can settle on a why it allows us to name and put more language to our experience, to identify how we and others are impacted. This, in turn, activates the left side of our prefrontal cortex, our brain's "executive command center."

Research has shown that the left prefrontal cortex is associated with what's called our *approaching systems*—which can help us get curious about a situation and creative in our approach to resolving it. A right-hemisphere-dominant prefrontal cortex response is associated with our more defensive *avoidance systems*, which can prompt us to shut down, self-medicate, and run away.

We also know that trauma is stored in a nonlinear, noncoherent system called *implicit memory*, which accounts for the ways in which difficult memories (sometimes including entire childhoods) so often have holes and missing pieces to them. Thus, theoretical expositions on how and why we are the way that we are can help us to pull what's been tattered and torn in us out of implicit memory and into concious coherency. It can help bring the parts of us holding unprocessed emotional experiences out of fragmentation and into a place where emotions and narratives can finally flow. Simply put, when we are able to name the moving parts involved in an experience—especially when it's difficult—it can restore our sense of clarity and empowerment.

It is in this spirit of the healing power of theory that, in part 3, I'll expand our discussion to include insights from contemporary neuroscience, which align quite seamlessly with the parts work model we've been exploring. Learning about our brain systems and nervous systems can provide an incredibly helpful background in terms of understanding our psychological "parts." They are, aftera all, not just idiosyncratic, not just individual in nature but partly patterned responses to societal forces. Broadening out our view in this way facilitates turning our discussion in the direction of social structures and social conditioning. To this end, I'll be discussing some of the dynamic neuropsychological systems involved in the lived experience of social perception: namely, that our neurology and unconscious psychologies play an enormous role in matters of power, privilege, and injustice. I've found this way of looking at my own experience immensely helpful. Any increase in awareness fortifies our personal freedom because awareness always leads to choices. For people carrying a lot of trauma, this can mean having new options to reframe one's past and move forward with greater empowerment. For people carrying a lot of privilege (who might also be carrying a lot of trauma), this can mean perceiving more accurately—and over time, more quickly—how our neuropsychological tendencies and social conditioning lead us to deny, protect, and perpetuate our privilege. It can mean, instead, learning how to acknowledge our privilege, use it for good, and share it.

That said, I want to be careful to acknowledge that what I am offering are plausible theories based on what we know about the brain. I aim to help us identify some of the conditions involved, not to try to pin down causation. I approach these matters as an opportunity to raise awareness and to bring a different kind of precision to an ongoing discourse. To the best of my ability, I've tried to use language that isn't clinical or jargon-y, so as to keep things as accessible as possible. As a result, some of what I'm putting forth could be critiqued as reductive or apologist, especially by those who might read things out of context (as we are all prone to do). In my experience, to wade into waters such as race and oppression is a sure way to expose one's blind spots and conditioning. Yet to avoid such topics is to sidestep some of the most critical issues that inform not only our outer worlds but also our inner ones. So, into the waters I go. . . .

8 THE DEFENDER AND THE SAGE

Emotional Intelligence in the Context of
Active Traumatization and Oppression

Justice is what love looks like in public.
Tenderness is what love feels like in private.
—*Dr. Cornel West*

» **THE** natural world has much to teach us about the way life
works. Pay enough attention to the activity of the flora, fauna,
and seasons that surround us, and it's inevitable that insights
about our own life, relationships, and the nature of existence
will dawn. Relating to nonhuman animals can be especially
revealing when it comes to understanding our own motivations and processes. Our brains really aren't so different from
theirs. We all share an archaic limbic system, responsible for
our defensive fight-flight response. All primates also have a
neocortex, which is heavily involved in generating our more
elevated, socially connected, and decent sensibilities. The
main difference between humans and most other primates is
that we have a far more developed neocortex than they do.
Ever wonder why dogs have much more expressive person-
alities and even something resembling a sense of humor when

compared to cats? This is due, in part, to dogs having more developed neocortices. How strange that they—*ahem*—remain the inferior creature of the two. (I kid, I kid.)

If we are to understand anything about human behavior, we must understand that our brains and bodies aren't really designed for the twenty-first century. We are built to hunt and gather. We're more equipped for nomadic lifestyles. Our minds and bodies have all they need to address situations that are simpler and yet entail a much more severe precarity: identifying dangerous predators, finding adequate shelter, fending off other groups not known to ours. The emotional responses involved in such a life are far more intense than what most of us need to navigate our world today.

The limbic system, which is involved in all acts of aggression and violence, is basically a primitive being. For our purposes here, we'll refer to this part of our brain as "the Defender." The renowned neuropsychiatrist Dan Siegel once said during a training that when we get angry, we can think of the anger of a mother fish in a pond in a cave protecting her eggs from a predator 500 million years ago. We can consider the fight-flight mechanism our defensive parts employ as having the force of half a billion years of evolution behind it. It's ancient, but it is strong.

The neocortex is the seat of our compassion, morality, willpower, personality, and problem-solving ability, as well as our senses of identity and connection to others. It's a little closer to a Buddha—gentle enough to appreciate the innate preciousness of all human life and connect with others, strong enough to weather stormy seas. It's like a Sage—confident enough to assert itself and its worth, genuine enough to do the right thing even when nobody's watching. It's also, evolutionarily speaking, the youngest part of the brain. In other words, the sagely neocortex is yet to develop the sheer prowess that the Defender—the limbic system—enjoys. Though, in a functional sense, these two parts of the brain are tightly integrated, I find it helpful to delineate them to describe two polar opposite types of emotional responses.

No one has taught me more about these two types of emotional responses than Emma Goldman and Henry Lee, my two cats. (FYI, Henry Lee is named after the transcendent song by Nick Cave and PJ Harvey, *not* after the serial killer.) Most of the time, they're love machines. I challenge you to find cats more aggressively affectionate. It won't happen. Yet, I witness the strange metamorphosis they undergo every day in response to powerful and specific stimuli: even the slightest crinkling of a bag of cat treats, and they are transformed.

They'll be in their natural state—pacific, purring, affection-prone. Bring out the cat treats, though, and they become *los desperados*. Their Defenders light up. In a flash, they're edgy, pensive, anxious. They frantically consume at lightning speeds whatever I toss them. They also begin bullying each other, competing for more. And when treat time is over, they vigilantly scour the floor, just in case. You'd think I'd get some appreciation from them, being Gatekeeper of the Treats and all. But once treat time is over, should I try to pet them, they jump back away from me as if I'm a threat. When they finally realize that there are no more morsels to be had, they leave the room.

This used to confuse me to no end. In a flash, we go from a connected moment to a treat-induced mania, and then they turn against me. What gives?

SAFETY, REWARDS, AND BELONGING

At the neurological level, beings are driven by three basic things we need in order to thrive: safety, feel-good rewards, and belonging. These intrinsic, core motivations correlate with the three basic layers of the brain: brain stem, mid-brain, and neocortex. When we perceive that we are safe and our basic needs are seen to, the brain stem's basic functions are fulfilled. When we are in the presence of feel-good rewards—such as when we learn something new, engage in fulfilling work, or drive to the beach to enjoy the sun and the waves—the basic function of the midlayer of the brain is fulfilled. When we sense that we belong, when we connect with others, when we perceive that we are seen and valued and understood, the neocortex's fundamental function is fulfilled. Indeed, the hum of life that courses through each of us is constantly reaching in these directions, just like a plant will always grow toward the sun. Even those who express hatred and commit vile acts of violence believe they must do so in order to be safe (think white nationals chanting "Jews will not replace us!"), in order to be rewarded (think domestic and foreign terrorists believing they'll be favored in heaven), or to belong (think Charles Manson and his followers calling themselves "family").

Emma and Henry enjoy a baseline of having these needs fulfilled. They eat better than I do (safety), we play often (rewards), and many are the head boops that go on in my house (belonging). These conditions give rise to a nearly automatic mental state in them scientifically known as Love Machine. But make no mistake, as much as we humans like to fantasize about living the lifestyle of a housecat or dog, the life of an animal is an anxious one. Hardwired into these cats are their wilder instincts, ones designed to contend with tremendous insecurity and uncertainty. In the wild, carnivorous animals must hunt down and eat another being alive every time they get hungry. And they are under constant threat of being eaten alive themselves.

What's more, Henry and Emma are shelter cats who were rescued from the streets of New York City. Their earliest experiences involved the scarcity of food and the protection of shelter. Thus, their mental association with food—even with the indulgence of cat treats—is survival. They hear the rustle of any bag in the house that might be treats, and their Defenders come right out. In these moments, they are literally different beings—ambivalent to our connection, laser focused on one thing only: *Get the treats! Eat the treats! Treats!! Wait—no more treats? We're outta here. You're dead to us, dude.*

As the social reformer Dorothea Dix wrote, "No one wants to kiss when they're hungry."

Same thing with us humans. To the extent that we perceive that we're safe, that life feels basically good, and that we feel that we belong (which includes feeling relatively worthy, good enough, seen, heard, respected, and like we matter), we are free to abide in the Sage. When these fundamental needs aren't sufficiently met, however, we become stressed, and our evolutionarily ancient impulses are prone to take over. Stress literally hijacks us in an unconscious process that has no room for questioning or empathy. Rather, our brains begin to objectify beings and experiences into narrow binaries such as "safe versus unsafe" and "us versus them." In Internal Family Systems, some of the Defender parts of us are actually called "firefighters." You can think of such reactive defenses as swooping in, well-equipped to do a heroic job, but not having so much time to think. A building is burning, after all.

Please keep all this in mind as we walk through a true story (with all demographic information changed to protect confidentiality).

EMOTIONAL RESILIENCE IN
THE CONTEXT OF POVERTY

CONTENT WARNING: violence and death involving children

The neurological cost of continuous stress is why poverty is one of the most traumatizing conditions a person can live in. One never gets to leave survival mode. Although I cannot write from inside the deepest levels of experiencing poverty and racism, I must report what I saw in the days that I endeavored to be with people in such places. I am not exaggerating when I say it is perhaps the most radical and ubiquitous form of terrorism around. In all honesty, one part of me is including this story to help us understand the relationship between active adversity and our emotions. Another part of me sees that stories such as these must be moved out of the margins and to the center if we are serious about connecting our inner work with our concern for others.

For two years, child welfare work routinely took me into the housing projects of NYC. What I saw there dispelled any notion I had left that we live in an integrated society. Witnessing vast communities, almost entirely nonwhite, sectioned off into an alternate and unequal society blew the doors off of my academic understandings of how systemic oppression works. Don't get me wrong, I met plenty of people in the projects who embodied indefatigable faith and hope, who exuded love, showed me kindness, and celebrated life. Still, it's one thing to understand the concept of marginalization; it's another thing entirely to join with people in the margins they've been forced into; and quite another to be a foster care worker in their homes. Technically, I was there to help. Aspirationally, I was there to help. *Honestly*, I was yet another stranger who'd been given a whole lot of authority to dictate the outcome of their lives.

The police presence in the projects was heavy. Blindingly bright stadium lights surrounded many of the buildings and were left on all night. I learned there that emotional resilience for the good-hearted people I met most often did not look like cultivating mind-body awareness. It looked like trying to maintain their lives and families as best as they could while keeping their eyes open to the very real dangers all around them.

The first time I visited a family in my new role as a clinical foster care worker, the colleague I was training with informed me that a five-year-old girl had been murdered in a stairwell there just days prior. The killer was still at large. We knocked on the heavy steel door to the one-room apartment. A five-year-old girl we'll call Betty opened the door. She repeated the horrific news to us within minutes of our arrival. Her brother had been taken into foster care after their mother inappropriately disciplined him physically—and yet Betty was left to stay. The girl, very small for her age—possibly from stress or malnutrition or both—was perhaps the smartest and most talented of all the kids I came to know in this work. But her situation was such that her innate strengths almost inevitably came filtered through the toxicity of her environment.

Betty learned early on that the best defense was a good offense. She was highly manipulative, spoke in ways that could make a sailor blush, and was prone to physical aggression. At such a young age, she was already possessed of an uncanny ability to read people for their weak spots. Once, during a court-mandated supervised visitation (often a humiliating experience for all parties involved), she became violent and was restrained by my supervisor. Betty screamed at her, "You *cunt!* You never helped anybody a day in your life!" My supervisor looked up at me, mouth ajar. The little girl had homed in on the biggest insecurity a bleeding-heart social worker could possibly have, and she went for it. She got after it just like any extremely bright kid who'd been conditioned to understand that their survival was constantly at risk would. Betty's daily life had primed her for this.

Before we continue exploring the neuropsychology of our emotions in the context of active traumatization, there's something that simply must be said: children cannot make mistakes. Children cannot be wrong. They don't live in a mindset where right or wrong exist; none of us were born with that mindset. Rather, that's a mindset we adults impose on them. They live in a world of spontaneous, thought-free impulse. All any child is *ever* doing is exploring and spontaneously expressing the life force within them. They don't know what this world and this life are yet, and their only means of figuring it out is trial and error. Then they are conditioned by whether or not the result of their actions leads to—*guess what*—an increase in their subjective sense of safety, gratification, and belonging.

While it might be tempting to label Betty as a "problem child," as is so often done, such judgments are delusion. They are out of alignment with the truth of who and what we humans are, of the innate wisdom that we are born with and the wild ways it can be shaped. What Betty was up to was done without awareness or even volition, really. It was a matter of instinct driven by biological imperatives. As children, this was true for you and me, too, no matter what untruths we internalized.

WE ARE COMPELLED TO RECREATE TRAUMAS

In his book *Waking the Tiger*, Peter Levine, perhaps the most important trauma theorist on the planet, tells the story of watching baby cheetah cubs being chased by a predatory lion on TV. The adult lion found the cubs while mama cheetah was out fetching lunch for them. The lion gave chase and was faster than the cubs, but the cubs were more agile. They managed to escape the predator by zigzagging back and forth, throwing the speedy lion off course. The cubs eventually made their way up a tree too flimsy for the heavy, adult predator to climb, and thus secured their survival.

What happened next, though, is most telling. Once the threatening beast was gone, the cubs came down out of the tree and *reenacted* what they had just been through. They took turns, one of them playing the predator while the other child-cheetahs zigzagged away from the play-lion and up the tree. Over and over again they rehearsed and *relived* this experience, which we can plausibly conclude produced two crucial benefits. For one, it gave them an avenue with which to discharge the intense stress of almost being eaten alive. And, two: they used the stress productively—to rehearse their important new survival skill. The stress produced by the terrifying experience ends up serving an exceptionally adaptive purpose.

When it comes to us human animals—whether we live in developmental housing or in a mansion—we are biologically compelled to repeat traumatic experiences. It's crucial to understand that not all stress turns into *traumatic* stress and not all traumatic stress becomes *post-traumatic stress disorder*. What happens in the aftermath of intense adverse experience plays an enormous role in determining how it all consolidates into the nervous system. If we can discharge the stress, make meaning of it (such as when justice is served), be validated and empathically honored in the wake of the experience, it changes how the event comes to live in the body. If we are, however, met with judgment, told it's our fault, or told we're making it up or exaggerating, then the event is likely to take hold in the body in a very different way. If we have to walk down the street being catcalled every day, struggle with being differently abled, are made to live in poverty and surrounded by violence, or deal with other ongoing stressors in the wake of traumatic experience, it increases the likelihood that the experience will result in acute traumatic stress or PTSD.

All of this leads me to the question: Where in our so-called human civilization do we have places where we can discharge the stress of such frightening experiences? To go and make meaning of them? To speak the truth about those experiences and be empathized with, met with open arms? Most privileged people have a hard time finding such warm places to land in our world, not to speak of a five-year-old girl of color in the NYC housing projects. Thus, where else does this natural instinct to repeat what has terrified us have to express itself? If you had any judgment about Betty and her behavior before, I urge you to go back and reread the brief synopsis of her story now.

My express mission as a social worker—to help connect the mother to mental health and employment services, help her learn better parenting practices, and help her get out of poverty—turned out to be a fantasy. In the year and a half I worked with this family, nothing improved. Things only went backward. Betty's single mom was a POC lesbian woman who had herself grown up in the projects in the Bronx. She was a survivor of severe sexual abuse and a recovering alcoholic who had never received quality treatment for her trauma or addiction. How was she supposed to get a job when, in addition to her emotional turmoil, she had a daughter whom no babysitting services would take and a son on the autism spectrum separated from her in foster care? The foster care system demanded that she be available for twice-weekly supervised visits, endless court dates, and weekly home visits, as well as attending her kid's mental health appointments and attending her own weekly therapy and parenting classes. I've seen mothers lose their jobs over facing such demands. I've also seen parents not be able to get their kids back because they couldn't participate in this time-intensive, soul-draining process; they would have lost their jobs, and they had other kids to care for.

This woman also had no agency over when most of these things were scheduled, and *all* of these services were delivered by burned-out, underpaid, entry-level social workers. And after all that, she had to go home and try to take care of a highly aggressive little girl who knew all too well that her mother could not protect her from the desperation and violence often found in their surroundings. Neither of these beautiful, bright, funny, creative humans—so full of feeling and spark, just like you and I—stood a fighting chance of addressing their trauma and improving their situation, not to speak of bringing home their son and sibling from foster care.

This is one of up to fifteen cases I managed at that time. All of them were this complex and awful. There are currently about seventeen thousand cases similar to this one in NYC alone—the financial capital of the world.

^ ^ ^

The story of Betty and her family is of the type that tends to become polarized in our tense political discourse. You know where I stand on the issue, but I know that many others would read the story and draw entirely different conclusions—the wasted tax dollars associated with ineffective government programs, the steep price of broken families. What I want to highlight in the next chapter is precisely in this arena—not about stories themselves but about how we interpret stories. What happens in our minds when another person or group seems different, even seems to be inhabiting an alternate reality? By what neuropsychological mechanism does difference become a stimulus for bias and hatred?

9 WHY WE HATE

Deepening Our Understanding of Implicit Bias

We cannot lose our belonging to each other.
But we can forget it.
—*Brené Brown*

» JUST as a person breathing toxic air would find that in due time their lungs become toxic, it is impossible for us to live in a structurally racist, sexist, transphobic, and class-stratified society without internalizing the stereotypes we encounter about each other. This certainly plays a role in overt bigotry: consciously "other-ing" groups of people who don't resemble oneself or one's identified circle, and intentionally discriminating against them. It also results, universally and even against our will, in implicit bias. Implicit bias is the phenomenon of having subtle, unconscious feelings both for and against people and communities based on whether they resemble oneself or a group one identifies with.* Just as

---

* For much more on implicit bias, please visit the website of the Kirwan Institute for the Study of Race and Ethnicity at Ohio State University, http://kirwaninstitute.osu.edu.

someone breathing toxic air could dislike, speak out against, and act to change their toxic environment, yet their lungs would still absorb the toxicity, so, too, our internalization of implicit bias has nothing to do with our declared beliefs or values, no matter how fervently we hold them.

This necessarily means that we have all internalized notions from our culture of white supremacy, male supremacy, gender-normative supremacy, able-bodied supremacy, youth supremacy, conventional-beauty and anti-fatness supremacy, neurotypical supremacy, upper-class supremacy—the whole gamut. The structures of society live in each of us. It also means that none of us need to be hung up on trying to figure out whether or not we're racist, sexist, and so on anymore. We are. We all are. Case closed. And now we have some work to do, because we can root these internalized systems out. As such intentional change always begins with awareness (and awareness begins with knowledge and experience), so we begin our exploration here.

It's posited that some 70 to 90 percent of our mental processes are unconscious in nature. Our brains are processing data and deducing probabilities and possibilities in volumes and at speeds that our conscious awareness just doesn't have the capacity for. Yet despite the fact that our craniums house supercomputers that are more aware than we realize, the information we have to go on as we live our daily lives is actually very limited. The subjective sensory data available to us tells only the tiniest fraction of the story of what's objectively going on around us. Thus, our nervous systems are forever trying to fill in the blanks of what we don't know by reprocessing the information we have as well as repeatedly running probabilities and cost-benefit analyses of situations. It's a massive amount of brain activity, and it all boils down to trying to predict a future that is inherently unknowable so that we can safeguard our resources and bolster our chances of safety, feel-good rewards, and belonging.

When it comes to unconscious bias, the heart of the matter is perception. We humans tend to think, feel, and act like what we perceive is true. Many of us know that our subjective perceptions are highly fallible and inherently untrustworthy, and yet we still fall prey to thinking our take on reality is objective and correct. As Anais Nin famously wrote, though, "We don't see things as they are, we see them as we are." That is, in the moment we perceive someone or something, what we are perceiving has already been filtered by a number of complex processes governed by our neurobiological and psychological systems. In other words, we don't see things as they are, we see a facsimile of reality that's been heavily altered. It's much more like a connect-the-dots puzzle wherein the "dots" are the sensory data that we take in, and what fills in the gaps between dots (which are sometimes quite far apart) are hardwired biological instincts, social conditioning, familial conditioning, traumas, fantasies and hopes, and mood and disposition—for starters. If we consider how much information and experience goes into just one of these factors, such as familial conditioning, we start to get a glimpse of what a vast process perception is. We start to see that we are very likely to receive a connect-the-dots puzzle of a goat and turn it into, say, a zebra, whereas the person sitting right next to us might end up with a character from Harry Potter.

This chapter is about some of the "dot connectors" our brains utilize, without our knowing and without our permission, when it comes to implicit bias. This is not to rationalize or justify the implicit biases we all carry. Rather, it is stated with full awareness of our brain's plasticity, our inherent ability to change. Curiously enough, implicit and outright bias begins with something else neuroscience refers to as "biases." It begins with *biological* biases and astoundingly sophisticated tendencies that dynamically interact with our subjective psychologies *and then* with the world around us.

Unconscious bias, then, has everything to do with complex neurological response systems that intertwine with abusive social structures. Indeed, bias and bigotry begin to take shape in our minds long before we become aware of our felt reaction, and so it takes some education and some practice to make change at the deeper levels where we can undo bias at its roots. Although it is not necessary to know about the neurological underpinnings of bias in order to do that work—which might look as simple as spending more time communicating openly with people from unfamiliar groups—I do think that this kind of theory can help many of us in two ways.

Again, it demonstrates clearly that we have some work to do. Learning about the neuropsychological aspects of our tendency to bias can help those of us (*ahem*—white liberals) who think that reading the *New York Times* is enough to ensure one's progressive bona fides. It helps us see the difference between being *informed* about bias and being able to *perceive* our own inevitable tendency toward it.

Second, it helps lighten the sense of individual guilt or shame about the issue. None of us individually created implicit bias—it was here long before we were born—yet if we want to get free of it, for ourselves and others, it is our responsibility. We'll get more into how shame and guilt stunts our growth in these arenas in chapter 14.

This next section explores one plausible theory on how our brains connect dots—more specifically, how our nervous systems contribute to the phenomena of unconscious bias, the very root of outright bias. I want to be careful to say that what follows does not and cannot tell the whole story of all the variables involved. I offer no rationalizations for injustice here. Rather, I offer ideas and insights that I hope will serve as useful tools in our efforts to dig up the pernicious roots of bias.

DOT CONNECTOR NO. 1
The Storyteller: The Insular Cortex

One of our brain's main jobs is to take what we experience and construct a coherent and meaningful narrative out of it. There's a region of our brain that we're only beginning to understand, called the *insular cortex*, that's been shown to be heavily involved in this process. Actually, the insular cortex is mysteriously involved in a vast array of processes such as digestion, seizures, states of bliss and rapture, and notions of divinity, to name a few.

Researchers have found that when experimental subjects are confronted with problems that they can't seem to resolve, the storytelling insular cortex lights up and people are most likely to conclude either that the answer *must* be right around the corner, or that the answer is not inscrutable but simply lies with the will of God or the nature of the universe. Think about it: when something truly unexplainable happens, you'll hear two prevailing arguments:

1. "There must be a logical explanation somewhere."
2. "It's a miracle." (Or "It's meant to be," or "The universe is trying to teach me something.")

When it comes to the construction of meaning, the insular cortex seems to adhere to the maxim that uncertainty must be stamped out at all costs. It's a matter of survival, really. If we can't put together some story about what's going on, then we are less likely to be able to defend ourselves if something threatening is afoot.

DOT CONNECTOR NO. 2

The Pessimist: Negativity Bias

I just moved up to the mountains. I'm not sure if I believe in ghosts, but I think my new apartment might be haunted. At least that's what my insular cortex is telling me. I keep hearing noises downstairs at night even though the unit below me is vacant. The first night I heard the distinct sound of a door opening and I ran downstairs—with a steak knife of all things, only to find . . . nothing. A couple nights later, I heard the same sound, and in a flash I'm barreling down the stairs half naked with kitchen cutlery again. Nothing. It's probably a raccoon or some other miscreant animal foraging for food, but you better bet that if I hear the same sound again, I won't be taking that chance. If it's a raccoon and I'm wrong, no big deal. If it's an intruder and I'm wrong—*very big deal*. Those are odds I'm not playing against. My stake in the game is too high.

Same with our ancestors. Except, again, they lived amid much greater and more immediate threats. And, just like me and you, they didn't want to play the odds that the rustle outside their domicile was the wind and not a bear. Thus, we evolved to have what's called a negativity bias, an overarching tendency to run with a pessimistic interpretation of events unless we are certain it's safe to interpret our experience in a positive light. This is one of the reasons our limbic system is much easier to activate than our neocortical system. Our evolutionary training has conditioned us to take no chances when it comes to safety, but it doesn't provide much help in determining the actuality of the threat.

DOT CONNECTOR NO. 3

The Cult Follower: Confirmation Bias

In 1964, the Harvard professor Robert Rosenthal wanted to see what would happen if teachers' expectations of their students were altered by manipulating test-score information teachers received about the students. He administered a standardized IQ test to children at a school in the city of South San Francisco—except he changed the covers of the tests so that they read "Harvard Test of Inflected Acquisition," and he told teachers that the test would identify students with exceptional potential. He then picked several children completely at random and notified their teachers that these children had tested in a way that identified them as burgeoning geniuses who would experience a significant increase in their IQ in the coming years.

Rosenthal followed the children for two years and found that, when compared to their classmates, these children did indeed experience greater gains in IQ. As he had controlled for other variables, he determined that this outcome was due to the change in teachers' perceptions and expectations of the students who had been randomly singled out. Digging a bit deeper, he found that the teachers consistently nodded, touched, and smiled at these kids more often than their classmates.

It's been said that "seeing is believing," but, for our brains, it actually works the other way around. Believing is seeing. Whatever it is that we believe to be the case, our brains set about looking for evidence that confirms it. If we hold the belief that our group of people is special, for example, we are likely going to find some facts that confirm our claim. If I then go about treating members of my group as special, it's likely to bring out the very best in them, and thus redouble the confirmation of my belief. If I hold the belief that another group is unsavory, it's likely I can develop evidence to fit my narrative. If I then go about treating people from that group as if they are unsavory, it's likely to elicit reactions from them that I can further use to support my negative narrative about them.

The truth is, we don't perceive so much as we infer, and we prefer to infer what already makes sense to us. We all have an inner "cult follower" whose job is to find evidence that what we believe is true.

DOT CONNECTOR NO. 4

Defenders United . . . Against Vulnerability

So, our defense systems must tell a story, *and* those stories err on the side of pessimism, *and* our defenders are also expert at finding reasons why we ought to be pessimistic—and this is where our trouble with people from so-called other groups begins. To consider the notion of equality is to consider that we all exist together on a horizontal plane—on the ground level. From a survival standpoint, it's much better to construct a perception of reality that is vertical and where there's inequality and hierarchy. In such a hierarchical construct of reality, one can conceive of oneself as being high in the turret of a castle, confirmed in one's sense of belonging to the group that runs the castle, safe from anyone sketchy down below, and able to look out on the horizon to anticipate anyone approaching to attack. Me up here, you down there.

Thus, should, for example, an undocumented immigrant family from Mexico or South America begin to scale the walls of our turret, reaching for our metaphorical window by asking to be treated with decency and respect—at the level of our nervous system, that's potentially terrifying. Especially if our perception has been conditioned by news networks and world leaders repeating messages that those turret-climbers are likely to be members of drug cartels and rapists. Especially if we also failed to fact-check the person who told us that. Really, when *any* less-privileged group begins claiming their power and demanding to be treated equally, the privileged will be prone to feeling that they themselves are being oppressed.

Equality is inherently vulnerable—it's a social state in which we must come down from our turret, look other people in the face, and be willing to see the world through their eyes. It entails opening ourselves to meaningful connection, and that means being available enough to be changed by others' experiences and worldviews. It means the possibility of feeling one of the most vulnerable and tender things a human can feel: that we're wrong, that our constructed perception of reality has failed us. This is why we identify the role fear plays in bias with labels such as trans*phobia* and xeno*phobia*. Homophobia, for example, is a defensive response to the sense that homosexuality is a fearsome threat in some way. We've all heard someone say, "I'm cool with gay people so long as they keep it to themselves." This is tantamount to saying, "I don't feel threatened by gay people until I'm reminded that they exist, they matter, and have lives they must live in public just as much as I do."

Perhaps the most basic and fundamental lesson to be learned from contemporary politics is that reality can be bent. Perception is incredibly malleable. Two people can be standing side-by-side looking at the exact same thing and be convinced that their incredibly different subjective interpretations of it are, in fact, objective in nature. This has been going on our whole lives, but with the implications looking more and more disastrous, we have never noticed it quite like this until now.

Here's the rub: Vulnerability *is* risky. It necessarily means opening ourselves to sensations we associate with danger and loss. Vulnerability is very rarely a position we'll take as a product of our unconscious and automatic tendencies; it is more often a conscious decision we must make because we begin to see it's in our own best interest. After all, what's more risky: opening ourselves to the inherent truth that all beings want safety, belonging, and basic happiness, and deserve equal treatment for life—or continuing down the path we're on now?

CONNECTING THE DOTS

Here's the neuropsychological equation:

> brains that are only capable of interpretation, not
> objective perception
> + intolerance of uncertainty and an imperative
> toward construing meaning
> + unconscious default to assuming threat
> + unconscious drive to find evidence for the
> meaning we construe
> + innate tendency toward negative interpretation of
> evidence
> + primitive, efficient defense systems to protect our
> vulnerability
> + presence of someone with traits other than what
> we're habituated to

= fight-flight response: the need to attack or get
  away from that person
aka implicit bias

This kind of theory has helped me to understand why I was beaten and harassed all throughout my school years. I didn't fit gender norms, and therefore I couldn't be safely categorized (decades later, I still can't seem to categorize my gender identity myself). Faced with someone like me, my bullies succumbed to all the tendencies I describe above—needing a story to tell about me, going for a negative one, finding as many details as necessary to bolster it, and rallying their inner and outer Defenders to punish me so as to confirm their story. Since I was "weird," I was taken as both threatening and vulnerable—an ideal object to attack—and it often seemed that anything I did was seen in these twin lights. When I'd react, I'd be told I needed to relax. When I'd protest, I'd be told it was my fault. When I developed acute mental health symptoms, I was often told that I was just looking for attention. With astonishing regularity, others would ascertain on my behalf that I *liked* negative attention and that was why I looked and behaved unconventionally. It got to be so confusing that I didn't even know what my own reality was anymore.

˄ ˄ ˄

The neuropsychological processes I describe in this chapter play out at the personal and interpersonal level, but I think it won't be hard for you to see how the proliferation of these patterns helps inform the macro-structural level as well. This isn't to say that working at the personal level is the only way to address implicit bias—far from it. Activism and policy change at the levels of neighborhoods, organizations, cities, states, and the federal government can all help remove the conditions—such as extreme wealth inequality, patriarchy, and racial segregation—in which implicit bias flourishes.

But in line with this book's empowerment model, looking at our own minds and relationships is something we can all do at any time. At the level of our relationships, perhaps the best way to root out bias is to get in community, and stay in community, with people who are demographically unlike oneself, whose bodies and identities and lives don't resemble our own—and then listen, empathize, ask questions, and step outside of our comfort zones. And as individuals, in order to intervene in the mechanisms that generate perception, we must work at the level of our neurology and psychology. This cannot be swept aside in favor of the other more concrete tasks that lie before us. For, any attempt to address societal systems without understanding the evolutionary neuropsychology of groups and individuals is unlikely to succeed in the long term. We are also likely to forever remain in a finger-pointing stance of trying to excise the cancer of marginalization "out there" in systems and other people without ever looking "in here" at the ways in which it lives in us. As such, I've offered contemplative practices at the end of part 3 designed as opportunities for us to do self-work on this level.

Using the parts work approach evident in those practices and elsewhere in this book is an extremely practical way to start to approach our own implicit biases. We can begin to notice and label feelings in ourselves—some strong, some more subtle—that arise in relation to people who are unlike us. And we can invite those feelings into dialogue—asking them questions, finding out what jobs they are trying to do, and discerning whether those jobs are being done skillfully.

10 THE NEUROPSYCHOLOGY OF IDENTITY POLITICS

Why Embracing Who and What You Are Matters

» **EVERY** morning I adorn my wrist with three small *malas* (prayer beads). I've worn these for decades now, and with a specific intent—just not the one most people assume. They haven't been blessed by a guru, and they aren't particularly sacred to me. In fact, they're sorta dispensable—they break all the time. I don't wear them to look cool; frankly, they get in my way. I wear them for one reason and one reason only: identity. To declare to myself who I am: a spiritual practitioner. To remind me of my deeper nature and my aspiration to continually open to that.

It might seem redundant to need a visible reminder of my own identity. You may have also noticed, though, that maintaining a daily meditation practice is tough. Few who try actually pull it off. It's uncanny how obstacles "just happen" to proliferate when one commits to, well, anything challenging: how often we resist the things we want. And even when we do succeed in periods of daily practice, it can seem a Sisyphean task as the stress and tumult of the world repeatedly roll back the benefits our meditation has engendered. Well, I don't give myself the option of bailing out. My convictions are too deep, and the experiences I've had with the process of awakening have spoken too clearly to me. And, anyway, my mental health issues make it such that skipping more than a day of meditation is likely to make me a person that neither you nor I want to be around. So, I'm down to ride. I'm always down with bitter medicine when it's worth it. And this long-term relationship I'm in with daily meditation is beyond worth it.

But committing to daily practice doesn't eliminate any of the obstacles or counteracting forces I just mentioned. I struggle just like anyone else to sit my ass down each morning. I need all the help I can get when it comes to cutting through my excuses. Perhaps my most powerful ally in the maintenance of day-in-day-out practice, study, and self-questioning is that it's an identity for me. I'm a spiritual practitioner. Period. This does not waver. Thus, right there on my left wrist, cumbersome and too trendy for my taste, are the visual adornments that remind me of my relationship to the unseen world. It's my way of planting a flag. And, with that flag on display, I'm more likely to follow through. Something about it helps me to get past the obstacles.

But it's not some magical or divine causation at play. Far from it. As we have seen, belonging is one of our fundamental needs as people. When we sense belonging, it lights up our prefrontal cortex, the part of the brain that gets involved when we're tenacious, when we resist the temptation to flake out on ourselves or our values. The prefrontal cortex is also involved in things called *distress tolerance* and *emotional-behavioral regulation,* which are academic ways of saying "the parts of us that can take the heat, stay cool and collected, and not freak out." The prefrontal cortex is also stimulated when we tune in to a sense of self, a sense of who we are and what really matters—which is easiest to do when we feel a sense of belonging to a particular community or group.

Thus, affirming parts of our identity speaks deeply to our neuropsychological heritage as human beings. It's worth learning to do it skillfully.

‸ ‸ ‸

"We talk loud. Our language is colorful. Our food is spicy. And when we get together, we like to dance the *merengue*. We like to move our hips in the same way our food has heat— with passion, with abandon. And you know why? Not so much because it's cute. Because it's what's kept us *alive*—through hard times, through times with no food, through colonization and genocide."

It's the end of a three-day "Undoing Racism" immersion, and I am exhausted from having my eyes opened so widely. For three days, we've been sitting and talking, about fifty of us from all walks of life, in one room, sharing our experiences. For three days, I've been sitting next to an African American man who, when the topic turned to our experiences with the police, shared that he had been pulled over seventeen (!) times in the last year and never given so much as a citation. He was the assistant vice principal of an elementary school who was vocal about his passion for being a role model for young black boys. The words above (paraphrased), about spicy food and spicy hips as a means of survival, were delivered by one of the event's facilitators, a woman of Puerto Rican descent and the first of her family to be born in the mainland US.

Listening to stories such as these over the course of three days, I began to understand the importance of questioning the complexities of my own ethnic and cultural heritages and identities. Why do I feel so much more aligned with aspects of Indian and Tibetan spiritual culture than with Mexican culture, even though I grew up in a Mexican home? Why do I feel even more estranged from the Dutch and German sides of my bloodlines? I didn't grow up with that side of the family, but was that really why? In the identity choices I made to try to survive and get by growing up in American culture, what did I leave behind? How does the fact that I'm light-skinned and "passable" as white factor into these questions? I get privilege for this, but being estranged from and confused about my cultural identity is also a pretty big loss. What messages about race, about Mexican-ness, both verbal and nonverbal, did I pick up when I was too young to question them? What powerful emotional forces came into play in my family that informed these messages?

I didn't feel a part of *any* ethnic culture, really, growing up. I might have been raised on beans and rice ten miles away from the Mexican border in a predominantly brown-skinned town, but the sense of belonging within Mexican culture somehow missed me. I've never *felt* Mexican. I didn't grow up with a sense of "these are my people"; I emerged from adolescence with a sense of "I don't really have people." I rejected any hint of mainstream culture, whether Mexican or American, in favor of embracing the dissonant subcultures of metal and punk music instead. The rejection included the country culture of my dad's side of the family due to the fact that I simply wasn't raised in his home state of Oklahoma and the experiences I did have there left me . . . well, burned.

What happened in terms of the Mexican side? What informed my own internalization of racism? Did I internalize racism after being a victim of gang violence by other adolescents who happened to be Mexican? Did I give up on everything because of the trauma of a decade and a half of physical and psychological violence I endured for refusing to conform to gender norms and exhibiting leadership qualities that made me stand out as "loud"? Or maybe it was that I had heard too many fables about Mexico—that I had better stay away from the border because I could be kidnapped or taken into custody by corrupt police should I cross over. Such myths, rooted in exception-to-the-rule actualities, abound in border-town cultures. Or maybe it had less to do with the supposed problems of Mexican culture than with the coercive gravitational pull that whiteness had on my family—as it has had on so many generations of American families of various races and ethnicities.

I have difficulty embracing my biracial POC status because of my light-skin privilege and because I don't consider myself to have ever suffered through racism. But then I consider how racism has indeed affected my family. Various members of my family go by the English version of their names, despite what's on their birth certificates, because they noticed they were treated better by others when they made the switch—especially if they were on the phone and no one could see them. Among the full-blooded, more noticeably Mexican members of my mom's side of the family, I can only imagine there was an internalized fear of discrimination at every step. I wonder how this may have trickled down to me in subtle and unsubtle ways.

In the end, I embraced punk subculture to survive the darkest days of living with PTSD and depression. Later, I embraced a spirituality with its roots firmly in Indian soil in order to heal. Taking on an identity that came from lineages I was not born into was indeed founded on a certain desperation. After all, to live with family trauma is to embody a constant feeling of being both homesick and homeless at the same time. I'm just happy I found something that did more than just get me through, that had an emotionally and spiritually transformational capacity. Honestly, it gave me something I needed that I'm not sure I would have found elsewhere. I *am* quite certain that my addiction would have killed me if not for spirituality.

And yet it's more complex than that. I can take off my beads. My family can't take off their brown skin. Neither can a South Asian person hailing from the region my beads came from. Although, as I've pointed out, all humans need forms of identity to belong to and to celebrate, not all forms of identity are accorded equal recognition, respect, or power. Quite the contrary—we are now in an overdue era of reckoning about identities that have been used to oppress, exploit, and degrade those considered outsiders.

To go further into this topic, we need to look at whiteness and the culture of white supremacy—and not just the obvious manifestations of it, such as the KKK or other white nationalist groups. We need to look at white supremacy in its appearance as the culture (socially) and the identity formation (individually) that takes it as normal and good for wealth, political power, institutional leadership, and social prestige to flow to white people at widely disproportionate rates from their demographic representation, while at the same time mostly refusing to acknowledge these realities.

Paradoxically, whiteness has become so taken for granted as what's normal and what sets the standards in our culture that white people are largely unable to see themselves as having a racial identity even while they belong to by far the most powerful race in the country. This is why it's so helpful for white people to look for "roots deeper than whiteness"—a sense of ethnicity tied to one's European ancestors, to the earth, to a spiritual tradition, or to whatever feels healthier and more holistic than whitewashed patriarchal consumer capitalism.

We all need forms of identity, social locations, aspects of ourselves that affirm our sense of belonging. Our brains need them, our bodies need them, our hearts need them. And when those identities have been, and are, under attack, and continue to be so, it is all the more reason to affirm them as important and worthy of celebration. To try to move directly from our world—a world in which racism, sexism, and homophobia have wreaked unspeakable damage and continue to hold enormous power—straight into a world in which identity differences are taken as unimportant is to bypass our lived reality. It's positing an imagined post-bigotry world as our ideal and then bypassing the difficult work of acknowledgment, deep listening, and restorative justice that would be necessary to get there. It's also disrespectful to the amazing richness and nuance that have developed in the cultures of marginalized peoples—often very directly as responses to the incredible pressures and even existential threats they have faced.

This is among the reasons for proclaiming, "Black lives matter": It invokes our need to belong *as we are*. It invites neuropsychological factors that correlate with emotional resilience. In the face of trauma, it can help one move from the limbic system sense of: *This is happening to me as an individual. Maybe it's random, or maybe it's my fault. I'm alone in it, and I'm not sure what to do . . .* to the humanized sense of *This is happening to us as a community. It's not random. This has been happening to my people for centuries. This is our struggle. Other people understand specifically what I'm going through. This makes me want to take action.*

Feel the difference? Our brains do. Our bodies do. And this difference is everything in terms of the way our brains and bodies respond to and process our experience. It impacts how someone on the receiving end of oppression goes on resisting psychic death.

This is why we need gay pride parades. This is why Cinco de Mayo needs to be celebrated in the streets in America. This is why trans visibility is crucial. This is why relative able-bodiedness needs to be factored into all that we do. This is why it's beautiful and also deeply complex that letters keep getting added to "LGBTQAI+". This is why homeless and poor people should not be subject to punitive laws and policies that try to ship them away or shepherd them out of sight. This is why we need safe spaces. This is why women-only spaces are necessary. This is why we ought to tolerate the minor inconvenience of augmenting language to be considerate of others. This is why we must learn to listen without defensiveness when we ourselves are called out by someone for our privilege or aggression.

When people proudly proclaim who and what they are, it's powerful. That is true for me, a privileged author trying to meditate every day so he doesn't succumb to a lifelong depression, and it's true for the families of Jason Harrison, Eric Garner, John Crawford III, Tamir Rice, Jeremy Reed, Phillip White, Freddie Gray, Sandra Bland, Michael Brown, Heather Heyer, Itali Marlowe, Briana "BB" Hill, and countless other people killed by senseless violence because of who and what they are.

INTERLUDE

Why Demographic Identity Awareness Belongs in Spiritual Culture

» IN the last chapters, we looked at the neuropsychology of implicit and unconscious bias and of identity affirmation through a very broad lens. In this interlude, I'd like to narrow down the focus to how matters of identity play out in spiritual communities. In such communities, one often finds a particular brand of bias—that is, bias against emotionality, against seeming unpeaceful, against sounding too "political."

I'll be focusing here primarily on Buddhist and other Eastern-influenced groups, as those are the communities I'm most involved in these days, but I know that similar biases exist in other spiritual and religious circles as well.

There's a lot of rich mythology in the Buddhist canon, but there are a few more contemporary myths itching to be debunked: namely, that the Buddha wasn't political, that spirituality and sociopolitical awareness and action don't mix, and that affirmative identity practices are misaligned with the view of absolute reality.

SAKYAMUNI WAS A PUNK ROCKER

The Buddha Sakyamuni, much like Jesus, lived in constant confrontation with sexism, classism, divisive materialism, and other forms of social alienation. First of all, the Buddha was *homeless*. To the luxuries of his princely birth and royal status, the Buddha said, "Nah." He chose to dwell in the wild instead. He then taught to people from the lowest, most reviled, "untouchable" castes of India, who were barred from learning and practicing spirituality. He was also inclusive of women who were (and still are, in many parts of South Asia) considered lower life forms.

I encountered this misogyny in my short-lived ashram days. It's why I left, quite frankly. Remember that stanza from the *mangal aarthi* I discussed in the introduction? That was chanted with the cis-men at the front of the temple and the cis-women standing in the back. This custom was upheld primarily because of the prevailing belief that women have less spiritual prowess than men do. It was taught, at times with relish—and this is verbatim—that "Women are the Big Gulp of the spiritual world, but men are the Double Gulp. Women have thirty-two ounces, and men have sixty-four, that's just the way it is." Thus, it is widely considered that a woman's best chances at enlightenment are to marry a chaste and pious man so as to ride his spiritual coattails into the Great Beyond. Confusingly enough, I was also told that this is why I needed to maintain celibacy and cut ties with all women; they would dilute my Double Gulp (thus: women needed me, but I needed to stay away from women?). If you're wondering how a self-aware feminist would last even the year that I did in these circumstances, well, I kept thinking to myself that, since ours was a transcendent affair, my politics needed to be kept separate. But that mind-story had a shelf life.

The traditional Vaishnava sect of Vedanta practitioners I was involved with has since changed these practices and has grown much quieter about these ridiculous and groundless claims. This progress came about because women demanded that their social position be honored equitably. Without that, they'd still be standing at the back, squinting to catch a glimpse of the deities Radha-Govinda on the shrine. Identity awareness belongs in spirituality, that is, unless we wanna backslide to 500 B.C.E.

The Buddha was aware of the dehumanizing nature of many of the social structures around him and saw that true spirituality necessarily entails claiming our full humanity. Many Buddhist scriptures find the Buddha admonishing his disciples to rebuke societal norms, including participation in the materialism of the marketplace and the traditional family values of his time. He was so disruptive to the ruling orthodoxy that when the Bhagavad Gita (the scripture perhaps most central to Vedic religion, which had been passed down orally for millennia) was finally written down, there's evidence that it was done so in an effort to fortify the oppressive societal norms that Buddhism had people questioning.

In Buddhist circles, there are those who hold that any kind of identity affirmation is erroneous. Buddhist practitioners have been heard to say things along the following lines:

» "Focusing on identity just solidifies a false sense of self. Our concern is transcendence."
» "There's no race or gender in the realm of emptiness."

» "This world is *samsara* (a cycle of suffering), and we'll never fix it; we can only work for our individual liberation."

Eastern spiritual ideas about emptiness, karma, and transcendence have also mixed widely into the broad mainstream of Western nondenominational spirituality. There one can find many variations of ideas and attitudes such as "We're all one," "People are people," and "Love is colorblind."

It's true: it's all one. It's also true: there are many. It's true: we are not these bodies; our true nature is something beyond them. It's also true: we *are* these bodies; the body is both the seat of our deeper nature and the vehicle we use to uncover that deeper nature. It's true: suffering is inherent in this world, and, ultimately, we're not going to change that (sickness and death ain't going nowhere). It's simultaneously very, very, very true: the key to personal liberation lies in compassion, and this is, paradoxically and unavoidably, an *interpersonal* situation. This is observable in what many take to be the Buddha's most foundational and fundamental teaching, the Eightfold Path. Below, I've italicized the four elements of that path that are interpersonal and relational in nature:

1. Right view
2. Right intention
3. *Right speech*
4. *Right action*
5. *Right livelihood*
6. *Right effort*
7. Right mindfulness
8. Right meditation

Our interdependence with each other is such that our personal freedom literally *requires* that we work with the subjective suffering of all beings. And this means taking others seriously where they're at. Compassion entails recognizing that you and the other person's worlds are bound up together, and that their struggle is your struggle—is *our* struggle. How on earth could we privileged practitioners apply ourselves to this practice authentically without a basic openness to seeing the world through the eyes of those who live in the margins? No transformative empathy, no liberating compassion, no penetrating realization of the interdependence of *shunyata* (essential openness) can arise when we are so quick to shut down the conversation.

These are paradoxes that ask to us leave behind an ordinary way of thinking about our lives and open to a mindset that's much richer and less easy to grasp.

In Buddhism there are volumes of teachings on the nature of both absolute reality and relative reality. To say that "it's all one," or "skin color is an illusion," or "gender identity affirms a false notion of self," or "we are here to transcend mundane problems such as politics"—these are truths that are connected to the nature of absolute reality. They are truths regarding the energetic substratum of material existence. Core to this understanding, however, is that the relative realm—this earthly existence where things are *not* one, where racial and gender identity do exist, and where our lives are undoubtedly caught in the mire of politics—is just as real and meaningful to our practice as the absolute is. Deep teachings on absolute reality are always careful to state that both of these realities are occurring simultaneously and that we must tend to both. We are confoundingly and simultaneously working to identify with our deeper nature of Buddhahood and must relate to all that's connected to the fictitious earthbound identity. This is as inclusive of matters such as race and gender as it is our need to tend to the dishes and laundry. To be a spiritual practitioner is to strive to have an excellent relationship to the absolute and an excellent relationship to the relative world at the same time.

I delight in a Hindu mantra that perfectly crystalizes the matter: *achintya-bheda-abheda-tattva.* It means, "the inconceivable truth of our existence is simultaneous unity and plurality, difference and nondifference, sameness and diversity." It points us to the way the sacred and the mundane are dancing with one another, the transcendent and the ordinary forever locked in a tango.

Who we are is beyond this world and in this world at the exact same time. Our true nature is beyond the limited ideas of personhood or "being somebody" to which we've been conditioned in our lives. In a sense, our true nature is a "nobody." But to paraphrase Ram Dass: you've got to know you're somebody before you realize you're nobody. And that cycle of being somebody and being nobody is one that will continue as long as we are alive. Our mission is to get good at being both.

PART THREE PRACTICES

» Heart Breathing

Decide how long you'll practice this for and set a timer. Take some moments to organize your posture so that you are sitting upright, balanced, and relaxed. Begin to engage in the belly breathing just as you did in the "Grounding: Body of Breath" practice on page 94. Breath in through the nose or mouth, and out through the mouth. Allow the breath to find its way down into the furthest reaches of the belly, below the navel. Allow the belly to delightfully expand on the inhale, and relax as it collapses on the exhale. Let the breath be slow, long, deep, and quiet.

After two or three minutes, expand the breath. After the belly is completely full, keep breathing and allow the breath to fill up the chest cavity, the arena of the heart. If it feels good, you can pause at the end of the inhale and enjoy feeling the body completely full of breath. You can also allow there to be a gentle pause at the end of the exhale of a few seconds where everything elegantly stops for a beat. Continue for two to three minutes.

Let go of the deep breathing and appreciate the sense of space it's brought to the body. Let your awareness come to the center of your chest, the space of the heart, and pretend that your nose is there in the heartspace. Begin to breathe into the heart, and out from the heart, feeling it rise and fall as you do so.

As you heart-breathe, notice what thoughts, sensations in the body, emotions, sounds in the room, and other sensory stimuli grab your attention. Instead of trying to shut all this out, breathe it in. As you inhale, imagine that your breath is like a tractor beam that is gathering absolutely everything in your experience into the space of the heart. Gather it as deeply into the heart as you can, all the way into your backbone *behind* the heart if you can. Gather it all in with each inhale. Then, as you exhale, just let go. Imagine the energy of what's been gathered in the heart simply unfurling and dispersing into the body—into your torso, pelvis, arms, legs, fingers, and toes.

This might take a few minutes to get the hang of, but just keep going. Keep breathing all that you notice in your outer and inner experience into the heartspace, and then feeling the release as you exhale. Rather than struggling with "distractions," gather them all in. Let them add to your concentration, to your vitality. And then let each exhale be almost like a sigh of relief, a break from all effort, a moment to simply appreciate the supreme gift of living in this human body. Continue until your timer goes off.

» Rewiring Unconscious Bias

Let's start with the good news: We are absolutely capable of change. No matter how set in our ways. No matter where we are in life. The brain is plastic, malleable, constantly updating. So, the question isn't, Can we change? The question is, What changes do we want to make? The brain changes based on what we pay attention to, and it is drawn to pay attention to what's novel, personally relevant, or particularly intense. The following contemplation incorporates each of these principles.

Sit comfortably. Take a moment to settle into your body. Take a few deep breaths. Try not to rush through what comes next. Respect the deep matter you're addressing by taking your time and doing this earnestly.

Call into mind somebody that you enjoy being with. Think of the sound of their voice, the color of their hair, the curve of their smile, what they might be wearing. Imagine them sitting right across from you. Begin to think of some of the many good qualities they possess: their decency, their humor, how hard they work, the times you've shared, all that you identify with about them. Stay here for a while, lingering in an appreciation of this person's humanity.

Let's begin to consider some other things about this person that you enjoy. In particular, that they're just like you in very many ways. Just like you, they struggle sometimes. Just like you, they've been hurt, heartbroken, betrayed by others. Just like you, their life is complex, busy, hard to keep up with. Just like you, they have great dreams that fill them with an insatiable longing. Just like you, they sometimes feel that they aren't good enough or don't have what it takes to be worthy of the life they truly want. They struggle with their sense of direction. They struggle in intimate relationships. They also love. They also laugh. They, just like you, long to live the good life—whatever their version of that is—and to avoid pain, distress, failure, and anguish. They are, in just about every way, just like you. It's frankly quite beautiful to acknowledge this so deeply. Send them a little love here. Send out an energetic wish that they're well, happy, and at ease. Notice what it feels like to do that.

When you're ready, take a few breaths and let this person dissolve into mist.

Now, think of someone you consider to be not like you. Ideally, it's someone whose culture you've spent little time immersed in. They might be a different race or from another country. They might be trans. They might be intersex. They might be gay or bi. They might practice a religion you don't really "get." They might have a higher or lower standard of living than you do. They might have no job. They might have a health issue like cancer or AIDS. They might have a body that's different in another way, such as a face that's shaped unconventionally, a missing limb. They might live in a wheelchair. They might be fat. Maybe they do drugs. They might seem "other" to you for another reason.

Pick your person. It doesn't have to be the "perfect" person for you to work with. Anyone you don't really "get" so much will do. Think about what they look like, the sound of their voice, the color of their hair, the curve of their smile, their body, their skin, their general demeanor, what they might be wearing. Imagine them sitting right next to you . . . close.

Allow your reactions to come to the surface. This is a nonjudgmental space and it's also private. It's safe here to admit any aversion, disliking, fear, judgment, even disgust you might feel here. It can be troubling to admit such feelings to ourselves, but we can't and won't change unless we get honest about what's going on. So, let it come. Let all the feelings and thoughts and perceptions you have about this person come.

Just like before, we'll begin to consider some other things about this person that are strikingly similar to the life you lead. They're just like you in very many ways. Just like you, they struggle sometimes. Just like you, they've been hurt, heartbroken, betrayed by others. Just like you, their life is complex, busy, hard to keep up with. Just like you, they have great dreams that fill them with an insatiable longing. Just like you, they sometimes feel that they aren't good enough or don't have what it takes to be worthy of the life they truly want. They struggle with their sense of direction. They struggle in intimate relationships. They also love. They also laugh. They, just like you, long to live the good life—whatever their version of that is—and to avoid pain, distress, failure, and anguish. They are, in just about every way, just like you. They deserve just as much respect as you do. They deserve to sit at the same table as you.

Stay here. Notice what's shifting in you. You might feel more aversion, you might have softened a bit. It's okay. Stay here.

If you feel averse. Can you become curious about the direct experience of the aversion? Don't get into the mental story you have about this person or why you're averse or why you're a bad person. Just set that aside. What is the experience of the aversion itself like? What is it like in your body? Is it heavy? Is it tight? Is it in a particular place? Get curious about the feelings you're having and stay there with them. There is no goal here other than to be curious and to stay present with this. Breathe into the sensations of the body or the emotions. Stay here. Over time, you'll begin to learn things from the staying. The feeling will begin to shift. It's good that you're being honest about this. We all have this problem. You're taking a big step toward addressing it.

If the feeling shifted. Send this person some love. Send out an energetic wish that they're well, happy, and at ease. Notice what it feels like to do that.

» Reflecting on Our Origins: Atonement, Gratitude, and Going Forth

Sit comfortably, take a few breaths, and settle in.

Take some time to consider just how many variables had to come together just for you to be here in this present moment. How did you acquire the resources to obtain this book? Consider all that had to be in order for you to be able-bodied enough and have the intellectual capacities to read or listen to and understand this book. Consider the infrastructure, the food, the water, the electricity, the raw materials of your housing, and so much more that had to come together for you to be here in this moment. Consider the trees that were cut down to produce this book—and the rain, sunlight, soil, and microorganisms that went into the growth of those trees. Consider the wisdom lineages of Buddhism, Hinduism, social justice movements, neuroscience, and psychology that were carefully developed over time, preserved, and handed down for generations (in the case of Buddhism and Hinduism, for millennia), in hopes that you—specifically you—might benefit in some way. Offer any feelings or words of gratitude that come to mind as you consider all of this vast inheritance.

Contemplate the indigenous people who once dwelt on the land you presently occupy. Do you know who they were? If not, maybe you could look that up after this practice. Consider that people's whole lives took place here, that generations of families lived here. Consider how they had to survive harsh winters—or summers, or both—and great adversity. Consider the food that was grown here. Consider what their pastimes might have been, what games their children played. Acknowledge the likelihood that a genocide took place, right here in this vicinity, and that we have benefited from that. Feel the remorse that may naturally arise from that. Offer gratitude that you are able to be where you are in relative safety.

Contemplate the role slave labor has played in the building of the infrastructure that surrounds you. The establishment of agriculture and a healthy economy. The building of railroads and bridges that made the transport of the raw materials that built your town or city possible. Consider that these people only did this labor out of mortal fear of unspeakable punishment and because they were utterly trapped. Consider that many of them died on the job, and that you benefit from that. Feel into any remorse that arises here. Honor it. Offer thanks from the heart for their unbelievable toil.

Contemplate the labor of undocumented immigrants, often grossly underpaid. If you live in the United States, it's very likely that you have been consuming food all week that undocumented immigrants picked, cleaned, packaged, and shipped. Consider that they paid taxes that support the infrastructure and economy where you live. Consider that they can never live without the fear of being deported—sent back, in many cases, to unlivable and life-threatening circumstances. Consider that they have parents and children and dreams of a good life, just like you do. Acknowledge the reality that many of them *will* be returned to circumstances that ensure torture and even death. Let the remorse and any other feelings you have about this arise. Thank them for their contribution to your well-being.

Finally, contemplate how your family came to live where you were born. Did your ancestors immigrate? Were they brought to your homeland involuntarily? What were the conditions? What was their land of origin? Contemplate what earlier generations of your family might have gone through living where they did at the time that they did. Have compassion for their struggle. Thank them for their contribution.

Seeing these things, how will you go out and live today? How will you acknowledge all your human and other-than-human relations and ancestors, and what kind of ancestor will you be to the beings of the future?

A TIME TO WORK IT OUT

11

WHEN THEY COME AT YOU THE WRONG WAY

How to Not Absorb the Gift of Someone Else's Awfulness

Living well is the best revenge.
—*George Herbert*

» **IN** parts 1 and 2 of this book, we began exploring parts work as a doorway to more creative and productive relationships with our own emotions. In part 3, we also applied neuroscientific and neuropsychological lenses in order to widen the view to include social issues. Hopefully it is clear from the practices at the end of part 3 that many of the approaches we can take to get to know our inner parts better are also helpful in deepening our insight into and connection with other people. In this final part of the book, we'll be synthesizing what we've used so far—parts work and neuroscience, working with our inner parts and with other people—as we look at certain kinds of challenging daily-life situations we all face.

The parts work approach opens the door to experiencing the incredible nuance and richness of our inner lives. Yet it would be naive to act as if emotions were just an individual affair, disconnected from the complexities of social conditions, outer relationships, and situational contexts. Perhaps the true power of parts work is that it helps us see what's alive in others more clearly as a result of our own inner excavations. How many of us fear that living with such openheartedness in the world means we'll then have to let all manner of toxic people into our close orbit? Or wonder about what to do when others come at us the wrong way? How do we keep feeding the sparks of fiery tenderness and tender fieriness when other people are out of line or just don't give a damn? How do we keep aiming high when they keep punching low? Does abiding in truth mean we cut off anyone we see abiding in ignorance? Does walking tall mean we purge our lives of all beings who don't reach for the same bar—or try to but not as hard as we think they ought to? What do we do when we ourselves stumble in error or find ourselves on Front Street?

Frank Herbert wrote, "The mystery of life is not a problem to be solved but up a reality to experience." And while he was clearly pointing to matters of a more existential variety, I believe this idea is germane to these interpersonal questions as well. I don't think there's a clear answer or that there can even be one. I think the point for us as intentional and ethical people is to wrestle with these questions and experiences for the sake of themselves, because it is simply right to. I think the point is to bring the light of a critical and openhearted awareness into these complex issues—not so much to find "the right way" but simply because the process of engagement is rich with lessons and fodder for growth. I think the point is to be as true to our convictions about the preciousness of life as we can be, to continually fail and fall down at times, and then to bounce back better than before. It's not a problem to be solved but rather a process to discover within. And we do this in the name of love, that which is also known as justice.

‣ ‣ ‣

There once lived a nun who meditated in a remote monastery for many years. One day, she finally uncovered the deep well of peace inside she had been seeking all along. Only, this wasn't some ordinary state of tranquility. The energy inside her was shimmering, warm, beautiful. The peace gave rise to a certain pull, a tug, a conviction right there in the center of her chest. It was as if the spaciousness of heart itself was longing to find an expression, to connect. The nun decided it was time to leave the monastery and to head into the nearest town. She said her farewells, packed her things, and set out to share her revelation with the world, with those who needed it.

The nun, beaming in her sublime state, walked until she found the perfect place to begin—an open-air bazaar. Only, having spent so long cloistered in the monastery, she felt jarred by the hustle and aggression of this place. One man knocked right into her as he passed by without stopping to apologize. Another man aggressively catcalled her. And while she was trying to shake off that experience, someone else told her to smile. The worker at the vegetable stand tried to charge her double for her groceries. A teenager attempted to pick her pockets. All around her, people rushed about fixated on their own affairs and wants, and the nun, who had thought she might act as something of a savior to these people, came undone.

Surprised, she reckoned, "The inner peace I had was beautiful, but it must not have been real. Genuine spaciousness of heart would not shrink so quickly in the face of aggression. True realization is unconditional, unshakable."

The nun returned to her meditation. This time she went deep into the mountains where she could sit with the trees and the animals and feel the warm sun and cool breeze on her face. Communing with the earth, perhaps the highest teacher of all, it wasn't long before the great inner peace reemerged.

She headed back to the marketplace. "I want to know if it's for real," she thought just as she passed an angry man walking in the other direction down the road. The man stopped her: "Excuse me—where is your husband?! Where are your children?! You stupid, selfish, childless nuns. You contribute nothing to society. You belong at home, tending to a household. I hate you and your kind."

He went on and on. And yet the nun found herself quite curious about him. She noticed his facial expressions, his gestures, a sense of anguish about him. She also noticed the sensations of fear and defensiveness in her own body, and she remained in touch with those feelings even as she listened closely. He continued berating her, but instead of reacting, she took in each word that he was saying, responding, "Oh . . . really? . . . How interesting you feel this way. Please, tell me more."

The man became even more infuriated. "Are you even listening to me?! I'm saying that I *hate* you."

"Oh yes, you've made that quite clear," she said. "But, let me ask you: Suppose I'm at home and I hear a knock at my door. I open the door and find someone wanting to come in, and I welcome them as a guest into my home. As the guest enters, I notice they're holding something in their hands. 'Here, I've brought you a gift,' they tell me. I look at the gift and decide that I don't really want it. And so, I tell them, 'Thank you so much, but no. I appreciate the offer, but I can't accept your gift.' Now, tell me, to whom does the gift belong?"

"It belongs to the guest, of course."

"Exactly! And in the same way, today I have welcomed you into my home, into my personal space, and I've listened to your words. And you truly are welcome here—but this gift of aggression and hatred you're offering me? I don't want it. It's yours to keep."

This allegory gives us an ideal model for how we can walk through this world as wakeful people. It reminds us that we can minimize how much aggression we absorb as we walk through the marketplace. And it suggests that we might have more options than we think we do in our dealings with others. The nun in the story has the composure not only to stay in touch with her inner parts—her sense of fear and defensiveness—but also to discern that the man accosting her is not *made* of anger. Anger, rather, is just a part of him—and a part that she is free to deny entry to. But all of this came down to one crucial skill: discernment. Discerning, aware, cognizant of whose emotions belong to whom—she is thus able to refuse the angry man's "gift" of hostility. She models a kind of mental muscle that is possible and important for us to build.

A client shared with me just the other day that, after hearing this story, she put a sticky note on her desk that reads:

Whose emotions are whose?
RETURN TO SENDER.

The nun's response is deeply counterintuitive. As we saw in our earlier discussion of neuropsychology, when faced with hostility our limbic systems tell us to get away from the angry person, to fight back, or to shut them out. Culturally, we've translated these impulses into conventional logic about how to handle interpersonal discomfort. Turn the earbuds up full volume, walk away, and maybe compose a rant about it on social media. The spiritualized version of this, I've been told, is to visualize a force field around myself that deflects any bad vibes that come my way. None of these are bad options necessarily, but each of them entails some sort of contraction, some sort of resistance to what the world naturally and persistently presents us with.

Those methods also entail quite a bit of emotional labor, something many of us are doing too much of already. The path the nun takes is different. She stays in her power. She stays connected to her body. She intentionally doesn't let the man rob her of her peace. She even welcomes him. And because she rightly discerns that the energy he is trying to offload on her is simply his own hostility, she doesn't take his words personally or wrestle with them in any way. She performs a relational jujitsu move that allows him to fall over from the momentum of his own anger. He comes at her, but she simply steps out of the way, and he ends up flat on his face.

That's the power of discernment.

⌃ ⌃ ⌃

I can think of a thousand instances of someone coming at me the wrong way where I accepted the gift. Where I didn't pause and remember, "Oh yeah—your bullshit doesn't have to become mine." In a flash, I take their vitriol and ignorance as if it were my problem and wrestle with it. Maybe I react and escalate the situation in the moment, maybe not—but I definitely let the person take up residence in my head. Even if I let it go for some time, there it'll be at 4 a.m. when I can't get back to sleep, eating at me. It's likely there'll be one thousand mental replays of the scenario (a conservative estimate), circling round and round. With each repetition, I'll think of a new clever comeback I wish I had thought of in the moment. I'll plot my revenge in a multitude of ways. I'll resent all the other times I've been in similar situations before. I'll generalize the episode in a number of ways: it becomes evidence that there is something wrong with men . . . New Yorkers . . . conservatives . . . some other group, or that life is inherently unfair, or that there must be something wrong with me "to keep attracting and manifesting this."

I'm the only one who does this, right?

From the perspective of neuroscience and experience-dependent neuroplasticity, this near-universal, all-too-habitual response is incredibly harmful. After all, the brain changes with every experience we have, and where we place our conscious attention heightens the way experience imprints itself on our neurology. Thus, each mental review of a conflict is wiring in the negative experience, like a groove in a record getting deeper and deeper. Also, the more personally we take an experience, the more intensely we're likely to feel about it, which engages even more parts of our brain. For example, if we complain repeatedly to our friends about what went down (as it is perfectly natural to do), we're then engaging a whole new range of neurological operations involved in social and linguistic functioning. Thus, we are not only deepening the neural pathways being carved into us, we are multiplying the number of neural pathways involved.

I'm not saying that it doesn't make sense to react. I'm not telling you to not confront negativity and harm when it comes your way. I'm not saying the nun would have been wrong if she had chosen to get out of there or scream for help. Part of me wishes the nun had done some actual jiujitsu on the guy. I am, rather, shining a light on a very sticky web many of us get caught in. I'm asking, what would change if we truly discerned whose emotional energy belongs to whom in such situations?

Discernment can drastically reduce the amount of precious time and energy we allow such interactions to drain from us. It can save us a few dozen (or hundred) trips on the mental merry-go-round of repetitious thought. One way to look at discernment is to view it as "having good boundaries," but I also like to see it as a matter of efficiency. There are a thousand different ways I can exert myself in an altruistic fashion. Every time someone else attempts to project their shitty feelings onto me and I bite the hook, it necessarily takes away from my other efforts to actually help. I could invest the time and energy to debate and argue on Facebook, or I could devote my finite resources to being there for people, organizing, and protesting in the streets. I could inch closer to burnout by confronting every little thing, or I could save my outrage for when it really matters.

Obviously, this is my truth. It doesn't have to be yours. Your calling and conviction very well may have a different shape. I don't, for example, feel called to get weighed down by the racist anger or comments of others online; I just want to continue supporting antiracist work. But maybe you feel it's important to stand up to such people and either confront or dialogue with them—or even troll on them. Still, how would the kind of intentional discernment we're talking about here change the shape of how you respond and the effects the encounter has on you?

The truth is, to be the angry man in the allegory would really stink. Anger is an anguish-ridden state to be in, and to get stuck there is a hell all its own. We are not punished for our sins; we're punished *by* them. To exert aggression on an innocent passerby is its own punishment. I'd hate to be that person, stuck in such ways. The truth remains that the angry man's contempt for the nun wasn't about the nun—he knew nothing about her. What's more, anger is a *secondary emotion*. It's always a response to pain (just as with compassion). Parts of us that hold anger and exhibit outwardly facing aggression are defensive in nature—and what we defend are our vulnerabilities: the parts of us that hold pain, shame, and fear. We can logically conclude that the man in the allegory necessarily had some sort of painful experience he clearly hadn't resolved and was still carrying with him. His angry parts wanted to make sure his vulnerabilities wouldn't be exposed, and so he preyed on someone he perceived as more vulnerable than he is, a nun, to exert this toxic sense of power. Seeing things in this way, the man we would ordinarily regard as an aggressor is someone worthy of our pity and compassion.

Most human behavior is an attempt to discharge what we're feeling. We are constantly trying to feel less alone with how things are for us. The more extreme the expression of our emotions, the more extreme the desperation to feel heard and understood deep down. We opt out of such habitual cycles when we take ownership of our own psychologies and know how to pause, process, and take responsibility for our emotions before we react.

12 WE GOTTA TALK

Navigating Difficult Conversations

> There is always a way for love to be in any
> situation, and that's by offering it. There's
> no circumstance where that's not possible.
> Sometimes it looks like sweetness and light,
> and sometimes it looks like, "I'm out."
> —*Susan Piver*

» **IT'S** time we learned the difference between being nice and being kind. The two are too often mistaken for each other, but they are actually quite distinct. "Nice" is about social correctness, maintaining a good face, sending your inner ambassadors to put on a show for everyone. Nice is what we use to cover up our deep-seated fear that we're unlikable, that there's something wrong with us, that we actually don't fit in. It's also often an adaptation to abuse when one has internalized a sense of "If I make the unpopular choice here, I just might get shunned, yelled at, or beaten." Nice is a mask that we wear. Nice is detached; it holds people at bay. Nice only knows the flavor of sweet. Nice is often a party to causing harm in some way. Nice is way overrated.

"Kind," on the other hand, isn't afraid to be unpopular. Kind puts what is ethical, moral, caring, and compassionate ahead of social propriety. Kind has a full flavor profile, ranging from sweet to savory to spicy. Kind prioritizes what's right and true over outcomes. Kind is more intimate, more vulnerable. Kind might be more difficult, but it's far more satisfying. Kind doesn't carry the icky residue of falseness. Kind isn't afraid to say no. Kind isn't afraid to, as the Buddha put it, "speak what is both true and useful." Kind isn't afraid of anything because it trusts that, come what may, it'll simply work with the situation.

In the previous chapter, we looked at emotional discernment, seeing how a parts work view allows us to perceive activated emotional parts in ourselves and others, and thus enhances our clarity and empowers our responses. But the story I used to illustrate that lesson, the allegory of the nun and the angry man, has a shortcoming: it's a story about a conflict between strangers. In most cases of tension or conflict—and certainly the most emotionally important cases—we're dealing with people with whom we have longer-term relationships: lovers, family members, coworkers, friends. So, in this chapter, we'll explore a parts work approach as it applies to something a bit trickier than a single instance of emotional jiujitsu—the art of the difficult conversation. That's the place where our capacity to put down "nice" and pick up "kind" truly gets put to the test.

GET CLEAR ON WHEN

You can use the acronym HALT to guide you as to when *not* to have difficult conversations. When you are *h*ungry, *a*ngry, *l*onely, or *t*ired, you simply are not likely to have the presence of mind and inner resources to remember your better intentions. A crucial aspect of navigating this sort of territory successfully is something called *cognitive flexibility*. It is reasonable to expect that, in difficult conversations, you are going to get triggered and feel the pull to lapse into old patterns of habitual reactivity. You can reasonably expect the situation to require you to be mentally agile enough to stay nonreactive and to remember your hard-earned mature communication skills. This is especially the case if approaching a conversation with someone you've historically found challenging. Use HALT as a rubric to gauge whether you have the presence of mind to pull it off as intended. If you're hungry, angry, hangry, lonely, overworked, or underslept, the conversation is most likely best left alone for now if possible. Few are the do-overs we get in this life. Don't stumble into this. Do it right.

GET CLEAR ON WHY

If you are headed into a situation that feels more like a minefield in a war and less like a family dinner or a diplomatic breakup or company meeting, get clear on why you're going there in the first place. We need to take ownership of the fact that we are stepping into the situation not out of compulsory obligation but because we are choosing to do so. Yes, the meeting at work is mandatory, but you are choosing your job. Yes, you may feel obligated to go to holiday dinner with your partner's family, but a sense of obligation is not the same as being forced to. You're a grown-up and you can say no. Yes, it would be more appropriate for you to have the break-up conversation or boundary-setting conversation or *whatever* difficult conversation in person, but, again, you have every right to have the conversation over e-mail or not at all. (And, yes, there are exceptions to the rules here.) So long as your decisions are kind and ethically sound, you are not responsible for the feelings that are generated on the other side of the situation. You are not obliged to accept the gift of anyone's awfulness. Life is hard, disappointments are inevitable, and, so long as your actions are kind and ethically sound, it is not on you if someone else hasn't learned how to properly deal with their own feelings yet.

You *are* on the hook for how and why you show up in the first place, so let's be very clear that you are choosing the situation.

GET CLEAR ON HOW

I'm a New Yorker who hates crowds. I get claustrophobic and edgy. I'm not the kind of person who can just put in earbuds and tune it all out. Those people are superheroes. I'm debilitatingly mortal. Still, if I want access to such an amazing city, there are simply times when I must endure situations that might as well come with the warning label "Instant Panic Attack: Just Add Water."

There's a grocery store in Union Square I used to frequent because it was the only place that had organic produce I could afford. Inside, it was like they had announced a diamond ring was hidden in one of the items on the shelves and everyone was frantically trying to find it. I'm barely exaggerating. I had this ritual: before walking in, I'd stop, breathe, and give myself a pep talk. I'd front-load the situation by declaring to myself that I was going to be patient, stay present, expect speediness and aggression from everyone around me, and maintain composure through it all.

The art of boundary setting and difficult conversations is all about front-loading. Having picked the time and gotten clear on the fact that you're choosing to walk into a given situation, it's essential to get clear on *how* you're going to walk into that situation. Who are you? Who do you aim to be in this world? What are your values? What sort of energy feels best for you to carry into interpersonal situations? Which parts of yourself are you inviting to lead the show, and which are you asking to wait in the wings this time?

My responses to all these questions can be broken down to two things: caring and integrity. When the energy of caring is what's informing my words and actions, that's when I feel the best. It's also when my social anxiety is at its lowest. As introverted and socially inept as I am, when I stop and remember that I'm really just showing up to share my warmth with others, group situations and other high-stakes interactions are much easier to approach. Generosity makes for a better social lubricant than liquor, it turns out. But we also need a strong backbone to support that intention.

GET CLEAR ON WHOM

At the end of his classes, my friend and teacher Ethan Nichtern has his students chant a vow to meditate every day for one week (and then they take the vow again the next week). He includes this catchy phrase in it: "I hereby commit—*for myself and no one else*—" It's a perceptive clause to include in such a commitment, as we often unconsciously expect others to fall in line with our aspirations. Say you found out some folks in the class weren't meditating at home, or that even the teacher skipped a day—it might be tempting to start flaking out on yourself. A less-than-empowered part of you might begin to capitalize on that as a rationale for not showing up. This is even more the case when it comes to walking through the world as a warrior of kindness. It can be quite tempting to go back on our values and our commitments when we are met with the somnambulistic tendencies of others.

It's logical enough to ask, "Why should I be kind when others are being aggressive?" I must, though, point out the reactionary mindset here. "What am I supposed to do, let people walk all over me?" is usually the follow-up question. And the answer is no. Hell no. We're literally discussing right at this moment how to not do that. We just want to be able to do that in a way that's aligned with who we truly are and aim to be in the world. And if we want to do that, we need to do it unconditionally. Our caring and integrity cannot be dependent on whether other people are kind or not. It must be for ourselves and no one else.

I sometimes do a practice I call "forgive everything." When I know someone is going to be acting with toxicity and I choose to be around them, I practice moment-by-moment letting go of what they say and the energy they're projecting into the environment. I forgive them over and over again, breathe, and continually recalibrate back to that sense of caring. And I do it for me. I care because that's what feels best. For myself and no one else.

Kindness is a bit selfish like that.

THE CHEESY SANDWICH

Having taken ownership of the situation, reminded ourselves of our kind intent, and acknowledged that we are not going to let anyone take that away from us, we're now ready to meet whatever the difficult conversation is. I'm going to give you a couple of formulas to use for the conversation to come. The basic and core formula is what I call "The Cheesy Sandwich."

It's more commonly known as "The Positivity Sandwich," but that's super cheesy so I changed it. Nevertheless, the idea here is to "sandwich" the difficult thing we have to say between two positive statements.

For example, a friend of yours has been taking liberties in your relationship for some time now. They lean on you for all kinds of things, and you're happy to be there for them, but you also notice that when you need them, they're less likely to show up or hear you out. You've been feeling some resentment for a while in the relationship and you now know that this is a sign of imbalance that can and will in due time kill the love and goodness in the friendship. Here's how the Cheesy Sandwich could go:

The bread: "Thanks so much for meeting me. I was thinking about our friendship just earlier and how much you mean to me. I love hanging out with you. I also wanted to open a conversation with you about some of the dynamics in our relationship."

The cheese: "I noticed the other day that when I came to you in crisis about x, y, and z, the conversation turned back to you and your situation before I even got to finish. I notice this happens pretty frequently and I don't know if you're aware of it. It makes a part of me feel like I'm not completely valued in our relationship."

The bread: "Don't get me wrong, I love talking to you and hearing about whatever is going on with you, and I'm hoping that we can evolve how we communicate a bit so that there's enough room for both of us."

ADDING BUFFERS

Personally, I struggle even getting to the Sandwich to begin with. The thought of it makes me want to dig a nice big hole in the ground and crawl right in. I fear the backlash. I fear saying the wrong thing. I fear getting so triggered and worked up that I overreact to something, as I am sometimes prone to doing. I've internalized the cultural norm of just sweeping such things under the rug and letting them fester until both parties are bitter and grow apart. I also see where fear is driving all of that. I'm deeply invested in being a good parent to my fearful parts, and good parents don't let their kids run the household. I've decided I prefer painful truths over pleasant lies. Honestly, there's nothing more absurd to me than running from the truth, whatever the cost. But since I know that my conditioning will suggest I avoid the conversation altogether, for me, I need more than the Sandwich. I front-load a couple more layers.

Before I even approach the Sandwich, I start with something benign and easy for me to say. Even though the Sandwich starts with something positive, I know that I'm doing the Sandwich, and even saying the positive thing makes me too nervous. So, I start with this:

"I need to open a conversation with you."

It's totally neutral, easy to say, and once I say it I can't back down. Then I follow it with an honest acknowledgment of my own humanity, which might go something like this:

"I'm actually a little nervous here. Conversations like this are challenging for me and something might come out the wrong way here. I might need to request a do-over if I fumble with my words. Just FYI."

Then I insert the Sandwich—basically:

"Here's what I appreciate about you. Here's what I need to address. Here's something else I appreciate about you."

Then I close with an invitation, like:

"I'm happy to hear any thoughts or even disagreements you have here."

THE TANGO

Vulnerability and defense dance together. Critiquing anything about anyone is highly likely to touch something vulnerable in them. It doesn't matter how loving you are, how solid your relationship is, or how rich of a history you have together; when we feel vulnerable, our prehistoric limbic neurological responses and defensive parts kick in and we become a different person. We lose reasoning capacity and we get tunnel vision; the context stops mattering. Our bodies take over, and, quite often, our defensive reactions become almost involuntary.

That said, we have two categories of defense systems: preemptive and reactive. Our preemptive defense system is pretty neutral: it helps us manage our lives like an administrator or an ambassador. Our reactive defense system is what gets called on when we feel too exposed in some way, and there's a sense of needing to get more extreme in order to maintain ourselves. Things like rage, numbness, and addictions are the domain of this system.

In charged conversations, you're 99 percent certain to meet with someone's defense system. The question is, which one? The one we *want* to meet, the defense system that is most likely to be amenable to a diplomatic and constructive outcome, is the preemptive system. When we start a conversation off with a neutral statement like "I need to open up a conversation with you," that person is going to get their guard up, but we're much more likely to meet with someone's ambassadors than we are if we start with "What you did yesterday really upset me." When you're approaching a difficult conversation, just visualize an inner ambassador and an inner defender in the other person, and use the Cheesy Sandwich to address yourself to the ambassador.

IN IMPOSSIBLE SITUATIONS

Of course, there are situations in which none of the above is applicable. There are situations in which you need to (at least temporarily) drop all pretense of mutuality and watch out for your safety. There are people who just aren't for you, and vice versa. There are situations in which no movement is possible because that's just where someone is at, for any number of reasons. But that's their gift, and you need not accept it. You don't have to participate at all. In impossible situations our only job is to make sure we walk away with our hearts still in alignment. There are times where all you can do is make sure you wake up respecting yourself in the morning. It might be unfortunate, it might be incredibly painful, it might leave someone high and dry, but sometimes, that's the only authentic option we have.

13 CALLED OUT OR CALLED IN?

Moving from Habitual to Intentional

To be heard, you must speak the
language of the one you want to listen.
—*Robin Wall Kimmerer*

» IN the previous two chapters we've looked at emotional discernment and navigating difficult conversations. Of course, such matters take on entirely new dimensions in social media comment threads and other internet-era locations where misunderstandings abound and reactivity tends to flourish. Approached with skill and empathy, though, such minefields can be turned into fields of opportunity for growth and understanding.

When someone disagrees with us, we tend to collapse our thinking into some variation of the following two explanations:

1. They just don't have all the information like I do—and if they did, they wouldn't be disagreeing with me.
2. There's something fundamentally wrong with that person.

As we saw in part 3, these kinds of reactions make a certain kind of sense from a neurological and evolutionary standpoint—they're defensive positions borne of our need to avoid vulnerability and to belong to a group we identify with. Whichever side of a disagreement we find ourselves on, it's very likely that some of our most deep-seated drives are getting activated and that the chance for authentic connection is quickly diminishing. This seems to be especially true of interactions that occur within the fantastically tone-deaf arena of social media, wherein empathy is so easily set out to sea and misinterpretations abound. Enter: call-out culture. A scourge to some, a necessary evil to others, a divinely given right to many.

In one sense, call-out culture is just the latest manifestation of deep evolutionary instincts, but in another, it's very new. We've been dealing with the precarity of social life since we were born. Call-outs on social media, not so much—for people born before the internet era, they're new, and for people born since then, there isn't an older generation to impart a set of best practices. But what if someone incredibly intelligent, evolved, and thoughtful could help us fast-forward to knowing *precisely* how to deal with it?

I went out and found that person. His name is Aaron Rose, and he's a spiritual teacher and transformative coach whose workshops on social media health, conflict, and call-out culture caught my eye on Instagram some time ago.[*] I had the fortunate opportunity to pick his effervescent brain on these matters.

Right out of the gate, Aaron reminded me of something I find it easy to forget: "Social media is *powerful*. Our words and activities online can (and do) have big impact." I know

* See www.aaronxrose.com or www.instagram.com/aaronxrose.

that I so often approach social media as a space of expression (as opposed to communication) and a place to let people know about my work. It was refreshing to be reminded, *no, this medium gives us immense power.* "Let's not forget that entire revolutions have been organized through Twitter." And that with power comes responsibility," says Aaron.

Turns out there are things we can do so that our online behavior more closely approximates our behavior (or at least our aspiration for our behavior) in the rest of our lives. In fact, Aaron has a *protocol* we can all follow should we be called out. He also has some awakened thoughts on a best practice for if we're called out and feel the other person is wrong, and another protocol for when we ourselves want to raise an issue with someone. I want to be clear that all the ideas and words set forth from here on in the chapter are Aaron's (except for where I've indicated they're mine).

A PROTOCOL FOR WHEN SOMEONE CALLS YOU OUT

BY AARON ROSE

How do you handle it when you're called out? Here's the most basic guideline: handle it in the same way you would handle anything else that triggers you.

1. Slow down and take a breath.
2. Remember that you don't have to respond right away. You're even allowed to turn off the comments on that conversation for a while, just to get some space. Responding while emotionally activated is almost guaranteed to generate more suffering.

3. If you *do* decide to respond right away, it might be best to say, "I received this, I'm taking some time to look at it, and I'll get back to you."

4. Consider this experience as education. Go from a place of "Life is happening *to* me" to a place of "Life is happening *for* me." Frame this as an opportunity to learn and to shift yourself from potentially being in unconscious bias to *definitely* being in conscious connection.

5. Remember that the experience you're having is of neutral value. It's not good or bad—your interpretation of it is everything.

6. How you respond is more about your energy and level of awareness than it is about what you actually say back. The central matter is whether or not you feel "in integrity." If you're getting feedback from somebody who's telling you you're being offensive, that's the time to ask yourself, "Am I in the right relationship with the person or people who are coming forward?"

7. Question your internal beliefs about the group or groups that the person who has called you out belongs to:

   » What were you taught about them growing up?
   » What behaviors toward that group did you see modeled by adults?
   » What would have happened if you were friends with them as a kid?
   » What would've happened if you had dated them?
   » If the two of you worked together, would you expect to be their boss or would you expect them to be *your* boss?
   » Ask yourself what might be unconsciously under the surface for you that leads you to feel a sense of separation from them.

» Ask yourself: Do I need to make amends with that group in some way?

    » Example: Maybe you need to have a "reparations plan" wherein you actively find ways to pay indigenous people back for their land, or African Americans back for their ancestors' labor. Such actions run deeper than what they might seem like on the surface. They're about bringing ourselves into a state of integration with ourselves wherein we're confident that we're doing the right thing, that we're in integrity.

    » Maybe we said something that we need to own and apologize for. What matters is, Can I look myself in their eyes in the mirror and trust that I'm doing the right thing?

    » At this point, what we say back isn't that important. If we're in this place where we've checked ourselves, the most loving words will be the ones that come out.

8. Consider it something you brought into your life for some reason. See it as an opportunity to deepen your growth.

˄ ˄ ˄

"Call-outs are simultaneously highly personal and totally impersonal. If you get called out for saying or writing something, then of course it's personal because you're the one who said or wrote it. And at the same time, there's a lot of free-form anger that needs to be released right now because people's voices have been suppressed for so long. There's often an impersonal aspect that's being projected onto us.

That said, just because we don't necessarily have to take it personally, we don't need to throw shade back at the other person for it, either.

"If you've done nothing, it doesn't necessarily mean you ought to take the call-out as fair—but can you remember to bring compassion and love to the situation? Can we have the generosity of heart to try to understand why someone is coming at us in the first place? What if, when we feel yelled at, instead of yelling back, we yell *with* them? One way to do this is to take in this person's rage and hurt and then go and do a primal scream in your backyard. Another option is to write in a journal about how upset you are about the condition of humanity.

"What if we allowed the other person's emotions to pass through us rather than act on our impulse to give the energy right back to them? In this way, we are doing our part in an energetic clearing that is happening right now as generations of suppressed dehumanization and anger get expressed, and injustices are addressed."

In psychodynamic psychology, there's a view that people unconsciously attract reflections of the wounds they most need to work on to feel whole. "You might be holding an unconscious belief that you and your work will be taken down, that your success isn't sustainable, that you don't deserve to be loved and supported for being who you are," Aaron told me, "and call-out culture just happens to be what's going on right now."

He went on to share a recent experience of someone commenting on his Instagram feed that, given his views on forgiveness, he clearly hasn't suffered trauma in his lifetime. "My first reaction was to give this person my trauma list," Aaron admitted. "But then I realized—that's exhausting." He landed instead on a more helpful interpretation: "This is just information for me around how much people are suffering out there and are confused about the concept of forgiveness. It's actually a reminder that it's something I need to keep teaching about."

The person in question continued to yell at him in his comment thread, and eventually Aaron decided to stop responding—*not* because he felt the other person was wrong but because he realized the person commenting would keep suffering in their anger so long as he kept being a stimulus to them. He says, "I felt *okay* about it," because he had thoroughly checked himself.

A PROTOCOL FOR WHEN YOU WANT TO CALL OUT SOMEONE ELSE

BY AARON ROSE

1. Get present. Identify the emotions you are feeling. Check in with your body.
2. Identify what you want from the situation. What outcome would feel positive to you? To feel heard, safe, validated, respected? For the other person to confirm that they have learned something from what you said?

(Okay, friends. This next one triggered *me* a bit, so hang on to your hats. . . .)

3. How can you give that outcome you want to yourself first? This will feel hard at first. It's quite counterintuitive, but it follows the following logic:

   » How can we expect anyone else to give us something we aren't already offering to ourselves?

» What happens outside of us is a reflection of something going on inside of us. If we want to feel heard, perhaps a good practice is to go sit in front of a mirror and say, "I see you. I love you."

You might be saying: "But I was the one who was wronged," and you might well be right. You might be thinking, "But I want this person to *change*. I want them to be *held accountable*." If this is you, know that I, too, had to sit with this idea for a beat. It felt at first like this step put more in a victim's lap. But then it struck me that wanting someone to change as a result of a call-out entails wanting them to hear us. It entails getting clear about whether we'd prefer to take revenge or to act in the way most likely to produce meaningful change. Step 3 in Aaron's protocol is actually deeply and psychologically savvy. It's designed to take us out of victim mentality and into a place of empowerment before we step toward a confrontation in which it would be very easy to slip into the stance of a victim, an aggressor, or some muddled combination of the two.

4. Respond to the situation from that place. "Imagine someone knocks right into someone else in a coffee shop," said Aaron. "How would a person with low self-esteem react to the situation?"

I know for myself that if I were feeling low and something like that happened, I might well fall down a victim mindset rabbit hole and start shooting emotional daggers at the other person for it. "But what if it were someone like Meryl Streep being bumped into?" Aaron asked. "Someone who's got their confidence down. She probably wouldn't even have to say anything—and not because she's famous, but because of how she carried herself. A person who holds themselves like Meryl Streep could probably just look at the person and know that they're out of alignment and need to say, 'Sorry.'

"Really all we need to do is say, 'I just want to let you know, that was out of line.' But the emotional place that we're in is going to impact the way that simple statement comes across, and thus the response we'll get."

NO ANSWERS

I'll be honest. My interview with Aaron prompted me to review many encounters I've had of this nature, and now I can see where I could have done better. I am in the process of reaching out and attempting to make some amends. We are standing on new ground together, and it's terrain no one knows exactly how to deal with. The universe is, in so many ways, asking us to jettison our habitual and reactive ways of interacting and to be in a new process of discovery together. We must embrace the pain involved in questioning ourselves, humbling ourselves, and honoring truths other than our own. There is no room for sleepwalking here. Presence is vital. So is mercy.

It's a topic with which we could fill an entire book. You may have noticed we didn't even delve into the reality of people losing jobs and entire careers due to call-outs and all the complexities present there. We have yet to discuss how we need a rubric, a system of measurement with room for gradients that we go by in such situations, rather than the binary of "you're in" versus "you're canceled." To paraphrase

Roxanne Gay, canceling misogynists fails to cancel misogyny. Canceling people does little to cancel the problem at large. This isn't to say that people guilty of violence, from the overt to the microaggressive, ought to run about consequence-free. Not at all. It is, rather, to admit that as strangers in a strange new land, no one truly knows exactly what to do or how to proceed yet. We are fumbling in the dark as we try to figure it out. May we learn to fumble with compassion.

14 CUTTING THROUGH PRIVILEGE GUILT

> The good we secure for ourselves is precarious
> and uncertain until it is secured for all of us and
> incorporated into our common life.
> —*Jane Addams*

> If you have come here to help me you are wasting
> your time, but if you have come because your
> liberation is bound up with mine, then let us work
> together.
> —*Lilla Watson*

» **THE** preceding epigraphs form an elegant one-two punch.
They demonstrate two truths that must go together. As Jane
Addams, the "godmother of social work," rightly states, we
must ensure the good fortune we so enjoy is shared by all;
to fail in doing so means we ourselves may just end up, for
example, on the receiving end of systemic abuse. The very
existence of poverty and warfare means we ourselves are
never truly safe from such threats.

Yet, this work cannot be done *vertically*—that is, with
a sense of "I up here will help you down there." Such hierarchical designations, even if only mental, subvert the
guiding values of equality and equity. Thus, the viewpoint

of the indigenous Murri artist Lilla Watson: despite the gaps between our level of privilege and another's, we must recognize our struggle as interdependent and united. It is a *horizontal* situation in which "helper" and "helped" exist on the same plane, even if playing different roles. We must recognize that not only does the existence of inequity mean that no one is safe, but also there is an even more immediate reality: privilege is corrosive to the privileged as well. It obscures our eyes from seeing the truth of our reality. Privilege lends itself to a certain manner of clinging to security that hardens our empathy. Such artificial comfort dampens the heart's creative spark and natural altruism. The excesses we've been conditioned to think of as essential suffocate the world and deplete its resources. We implicitly take part in corrupt and murderous situations with every sleepwalking step until we awaken and work to reverse it. And if you hold convictions regarding the laws of karma, well—our involvement in this situation is a really big deal.

Privilege guilt is of the vertical paradigm, and yet so many of us can't seem to shake it. It's a psychological position that is antithetical to its own good intentions, like a snake that eats its own tail. In my therapy practice, I commonly hear three narratives around privilege guilt:

1. How can I possibly embrace the good things and situations in my life when others are suffering? It feels wrong to enjoy myself. I *ought* to feel guilty for having these unearned advantages.
2. How can I justify the luxury of working with my neuroses and healing my own traumas when others have it worse? I should push my own stuff down and carry on.

3. Having it so good means I ought to work my fingers to the bone to help others. I deserve no rest. (This third one is subtler and is sometimes only observable in people's attitudes and behaviors rather than in what they report, but I see it in many people—myself included.)

I'll be addressing each of these narratives more specifically below, but first allow me to be direct: Privilege guilt is like flapping your arms to swim when you're drowning in a puddle of water that's three inches deep. It does nothing to address the situation—not for you and not for others. Just get up.

Funny how privilege guilt *starts* with an awareness of how others are suffering but *ends* with us fixating on ourselves. It's a trap. A trap disguised as a three-inch puddle. So, now that you're up, take a nice full belly breath, and please hear me when I say this one last time: We need you. We need the whole of you. We can't have you hanging out face-down in a kiddie pool of guilt. So, here's a towel to help you wipe off your face.

GETTING OFF THE SHAME TRAIN

Guilt is essentially remorse mixed with shame. Let's consider the terms a bit. In the way I speak about it, remorse is a good thing. Remorse is essential for the integrity of the heart. Remorse is what we feel when we behave in ways that contradict our own values and stated intentions, or when we carelessly cause harm. Remorse sees that what's happened isn't really acceptable, that we need to repair what's happened, and do our best to not repeat it. Remorse is uncomfortable and righteously so; our hardwired desire to avoid it helps our lives and our communities to function and thrive.

Remorse says, "This is not okay." Shame, however, says, "*I'm* not okay." Shame connotes that something unacceptable went down because there's something fundamentally wrong with us, and therefore we're powerless to meaningfully address it or avoid repeating it. Shame harbors an underlying assumption that there's something rotten at our core, something that will express itself no matter how hard we try to do better. Believing that something's intrinsically wrong with us, the parts of us holding shame can and will find evidence of our not-enough-ness in just about anything we think, say, or do. (For more on why this is the case, revisit the discussion of the power of confirmation bias on page 131.) As humans we contain multitudes, but shame tries to tar every part of us with the same brush.

Having parsed out the difference between remorse and shame, we're in a better position to see why the mixture of the two—guilt—so often gets associated with privilege. Let's start with the first half of the equation, call it *privilege remorse*.

We live in a world that is profoundly unequal in all kinds of unfair ways. There's inequality between the so-called first and third worlds; between countries, regions, states, cities, and neighborhoods; between families and individuals; between races; between genders; between species; and on and on. Let me take just one specific example—human hunger and malnutrition. In 2016, the United Nations Food and Agriculture Organization estimated that more than 10 percent of the world population suffered from chronic undernourishment.[9] The United States defense and war budget for 2019 was $686.1 billion. About one twentieth of that money could feed the entire world for a year.[10] And using money from the US defense budget wouldn't even be necessary if we just distributed food equitably, because globally we produce enough food to feed 10 billion people a year[11] in a world populated by 7.5 billion.[12]

If you are someone who benefits from unearned power or resources associated with inequality, and if that feels out of alignment with your values, then it's entirely reasonable that you might feel privilege remorse. And here's the good news—*remorse is actionable*. At this very moment, you could go sign a petition for change or give some money to charity. Or you could dig deeper (I hope you will)—you could go volunteer your time, start a nonprofit, or run for office. If some of your privilege feels inextricably tied in with your career path, you could literally change jobs. I'm not saying you should try to single-handedly revolutionize capitalism or end global sexism. I'm saying if you enjoy benefits from certain kinds of unearned privilege, take that remorse and pour it into something that addresses the mechanisms of privilege.

By contrast, *privilege shame* is not so actionable. Or rather, you can act on it for the rest of your life and never make an ounce of difference in the shame, since it's a kind of stable identity formation rather than a passing emotion. It's also likely to negatively inflect all of your efforts to help others, since the people you are trying to help (or the other people with you trying to help) will sense the hidden motive in your activity. Shame deepens the divide we often feel between ourselves and others. Remorse honors our inherent connection.

Privilege guilt is nothing more than self-hatred holding a sign at a rally. And self-hatred is a form of narcissism wherein we create the rationale to continue to focus on ourselves. For those of us with privilege, self-hatred helps us avoid doing the hard work of rooting out the ways we've internalized a very sick society. It's a sophisticated way of avoiding the changes we need to make to be right with ourselves and those around us. On some level, the parts of us that are scared of the scope of the problem get that flapping around in a kiddie pool is less painful than facing our situation more honestly.

Privilege guilt is good information. It's telling you something very important, although it's impossible to discern that important message so long as the remorse and the shame remain in a state of fusion. Shaking off the shame will likely also mean leaning into the remorse. There's a seed of wisdom within the neurosis of privilege guilt. That seed of the remorse that, yes, we ought to be doing something. We ought to be doing more.

If it feels like it's all too big, like addressing injustice feels like fighting back the forest fire with a broom, here's a way to cut through that: center your life on compassion. Make it your lifestyle. Live to give—to love and serve. If the thought of needing a certain result robs your motivation, ask that part of you if they could please step aside. Engage in compassionate acts for the sake of themselves. Do it for the pleasure of living in alignment with your own highest values.

You might even consider making compassionate action your full-time job. Is your job truly in line with your values? How does it feel to consider the effects your job has on the world? What effects does your company or organization have on the world? Does compassion have a home in your workplace? Have you been on the fence about a career change? Maybe it's time to get off the fence and choose something, anything, that will have significant impact.

I cannot tell you what a blessing it is to work in service of others' healing and growth. It saves me every day. It keeps me in touch with the pulse of compassion that lies at my core but so easily gets covered over by self-concern. Sitting with people who are suffering is difficult, but it is also an immense joy when I know I am being effective. There is no high on earth quite like it. Getting to witness change being made, little by little, as a result of compassionate effort is worth more than gold. It's worth more than security. It's worth every sacrifice. Take it from someone who, a decade and a half ago, having just kicked heroin for the last time, started with $400, a couch to sleep on, and no education—and now has the absolute thrill of helping at eye level with my fellow humans every day.

Should you find your true passion in the midst of things, it is my sincere belief that you will become unstoppable. You will align with the presence within yourself that is filled with the confidence of conviction that you can become like Jane Addams, Dorothy Day, Eleanor Roosevelt, James Baldwin, Caesar Chavez, or Greta Thunberg—people who have been able to establish global pillars of sanity and institutions that generate impact on a large scale.

USE IT TO DISRUPT IT

Now that we've spent some time considering privilege guilt in broad strokes, let's go back to those three narratives I mentioned at the outset of this chapter.

1. How can I possibly embrace the good things and situations in my life when others are suffering? It feels wrong to enjoy myself. I *ought* to feel guilty for having these unearned advantages.

Consider this: The logical response to having unearned power or resources is to use them to help those who have less of it. If you find yourself feeling remorse, take action, and see how it affects your feeling.

But if you suspect that your remorse is still carrying a residue of shame, here's a question that can help: What do you think someone who suffers more than you would say, feel, and do if they had what you had? During my time as a social worker, I often asked parents and teens in deeply complex and painful situations, "What would you do if none of this was in your way?" (Meaning: if you were out of poverty, able to get out of the foster care system, able to get out of the criminal justice system, able to get free of your psychological troubles.) Their answer would always be something along the lines of (A) I would enjoy it and (B) I would help out my family and others. To relish our good fortune and use the energy that gives us to address injustice: this is a recipe for a beautiful life.

2. How can I justify the luxury of working with my neuroses and healing my own traumas when others have it worse? I should push my own stuff down and carry on.

Consider this: Pushing our own pain and historical trauma down doesn't mean it goes away. All we accomplish with this attitude is submerging that pain into our nervous system— where it is bound to come out in other, more insidious ways through negative core beliefs and compulsive behaviors. It will eventually harm others for us to continue down this road. Directly or indirectly, we are always dealing with our woundings and reactive defense patterns. When we do the courageous work of meeting our subjective difficulties directly, it is a service to everyone.

3. Having it so good means I ought to work my fingers to the bone to help others. I deserve no rest.

Consider this: Loss of empathy is a primary symptom of burnout. A lack of compassion and consideration for yourself will only lead to a lack of compassion and consideration for others. Do you know how athletes develop the ability to accomplish extraordinary things? By working hard and then taking rest and then working hard and then taking rest, ad infinitum. Working hard creates the conditions for strength, but muscle and dexterity only grow during periods of rest and sleep. This is a biological truth and it is also a psychological truth. We need you healthy, well-rested, well-resourced, and enjoying life because we need your altruism and good-heartedness to be in this game for the long haul.

In chapter 10, I discussed the awesome power of identity to bolster our resilience, even in the face of dehumanization. Well, imagine taking on the identity of true change agent. Not just someone who donates to charity and signs online petitions but a boots-on-the-ground soldier for the underdog.

PART FOUR PRACTICES

» Developing Discernment

Imagine the last time you encountered a situation that felt confrontational or aggressive. Go ahead and let the movie play in your mind for a moment. What was said? What did they do? How did it make you feel? How did you react? Did your reaction escalate the situation in some way? Get honest for a moment.

Now, imagine the same situation, except this time imagine how, in your own way, you could emulate the nun from the story in chapter 11. Practice pausing and then take one full-body breath as you shift to discerning that the person coming at you the wrong way is actually suffering and trying to pass their pain on to you. Envision how you could welcome this person while holding the awareness that what's coming at you isn't yours. How could you respond with dispassion or healthy detachment? With curiosity? With empathy? With humor?

Now, repeat this scenario. See yourself acting as the nun in as many different ways as possible. Notice how it feels to do so; what it's like in your body? Make *that* feeling personal. Linger in it. Highlight and intensify it on purpose. Go ahead and exaggerate it in every way. This will help wire it into your neurology. Linger in it some more. The satisfaction and serenity that comes from such skillful action is the true gift in the situation. It's yours to keep.

» Lovingkindness for All Your Inner Children

Practice time: approximately 20 minutes

Take a few deep breaths and bring your awareness into your body. Just as you did in the practice in part 1, "Self-Love for a Part of You That Needs It Most," consider a moment in your childhood when things were sweet and pleasurable—again, even it if was a rare and passing moment of playing or connection (you can also just imagine yourself in a simple state of happiness as a child, even if you have no specific memory to work with). Call the image of that moment into mind. See your child face and eyes. Hear your child laugh. Get a bit curious and notice your approximate age and any other detail that comes to mind, including thoughts, narratives, sensations in the body, and emotions.

Then, imagine offering your child the energy of whatever positive regard you feel for them in this moment (openness, affection, calm, compassion). Just like before, offer them the good vibes you would offer a small child who'd been left in your care. Then, send them some sincere wishes for their well-being. Send them the thoughts "May you be happy. May you feel safe. May you feel free." Repeat these slowly at least a few times and imagine the energy of those words reaching them, lighting up their little face. You can send the words on breath, imagine them as a beam of light, or use any other concept that helps you get there.

You might feel nothing at first or you might feel a dramatic shift of some sort. Either way, just keep going.

We'll continue practicing for your child parts in this exact same manner. I'll offer fewer instructions to give you more space for practice and to follow your intuition. Please take your time.

Imagine yourself at four or five years old. It's okay if you don't have clear memories of yourself at this age or any of the ages we'll be practicing for. To the best of your ability imagine your face, your eyes, your smile. Remember what it was like to be in your body then, what it was like to be you.

If it's possible to get curious or feel some kind of friend-liness toward this little one, that's great. But even if not, imagine surrounding them in an energetic field of goodness and send them the thoughts "May you be happy. May you feel safe. May you feel free." Repeat these slowly at least a few times and imagine the energy of those words reaching them, affecting them.

Take a few full body breaths and let go of the five-year-old you.

Imagine yourself at eight years old. Same thing: see your child body and face as clearly as you can; feel your child presence. Recall what your life felt like at that time: at school, at home, with friends.

Surround your eight-year-old self with compassionate energy. Make it more real by emanating the mental-emotional wishes of "May you be happy. May you feel safe. May you feel free." Repeat these slowly at least a few times and notice their burdens lightening as you go. Breathe with them. Stay here for a couple minutes, repeating the phrases, holding space for all that arises.

Take some full body breaths. Pause and unblend. If you need to take a mini-break now or later on, please do so. Then, continue.

Imagine yourself at twelve years old. See and feel into the image of your preteen self as clearly as is possible for you. Remember what it was like to be in your twelve-year-old body, to be in your life at this time when many of us are forming our unique identity and developing deeper bonds with friends.

Surround your twelve-year-old self with that same com-passionate energy. Extend the wishes "May you be happy. May you feel safe. May you feel free." Continue for a couple of minutes, holding space for anything that needs to heal.

Repeat this for your sixteen-year-old self—seeing and feeling into what you and your life were like at this time of rapid growth and changes. Allow any emotions that are here to emerge (but not to the point of overwhelm) and be held in the space of compassion. Then, extend from the heart: "May you be happy. May you feel safe. May you feel free."

And then for your twenty-year-old self.

And then for any other ages you want to skip forward or backward to.

Take your time transitioning out of this practice. Take three full body breaths, breathing in as big as any of the emotions that are present and surrounding them with the breath.

Take one final moment to consider someone in your life who could use some healing. Dedicate your efforts to them. Wish for them to discover happiness, safety, and freedom alongside you.

CONCLUSION

Prajnaparamita, the goddess of transcendent wisdom, found herself locked in deep debate with the Buddha's closest student, Shariputra. Arguing their contrasting views of the nature of reality (openness and luminosity), Shariputra was no match. It is perhaps the most epic case of mansplaining in eternity—Shariputra attempting to outsmart the very embodiment of all there is to know. As Prajnaparamita continued to out-argue Shariputra, claiming one "checkmate" after another, Shariputra thought to take things to another level. He got personal, chauvinistic. Falling back on a widely held assumption of his day—that of male spiritual superiority—he attempted to invalidate the goddess based on her identity. He challenged her: "If you're so enlightened, then what are you doing in the body of a female? If you were truly realized, you would transform your body into male form." What Prajnaparamita did next conveys much about the radical, paradoxical, unfuckwithable nature of the awakened state: she used her supernatural powers to switch bodies with Shariputra. She was now in his male body, and Shariputra was now in Prajnaparamita's female body. Then, from the male body of Shariputra and with his own male voice, Prajnaparamita retorted: "If *you're* so enlightened then what are *you* doing in the body of a female?! Why don't you transform your body into a male one?" Shariputra, disheveled and disoriented, confoundingly caught, unable to transform back—and shocked at the sound of his female voice as he griped about it—admitted defeat.

* * *

Such divine mischief and poignant humor can be found throughout the classical texts and scriptures of both Buddhism and Hinduism. But this moment, found in the *Vimilakirti Sutra*, offers a matchless confrontation of sexism that goes down within the delivery of the deepest and most core teachings of Buddhism. This is not happenstance. Prajnaparamita, with an air not unlike the modern street artist Banksy, pulls a prank that lays bare the baseless, harmful, and sophomoric notion that the body she inhabits could somehow diminish her academic and spiritual prowess. And yet, simultaneous to that, she wordlessly insists that the body she has arrived in does matter. It is not random or fanciful that she manifests in female form. The mythos was recorded with intent. To document transcendent wisdom manifesting in the body of a woman amid a society deeply abusive and even murderous toward women was inherently meaningful.

The implications don't end there. Elegantly present within Prajnaparamita's story is much of the subject matter we've discussed in this book. First of all, it's pretty clear Prajnaparamita has some strong feelings about Shariputra's ignorant attitudes. Her retort is undeniably sharp, and yet her message remains crystal clear. She rightly discerns that Shariputra's awfulness needn't be accepted by her, and so she places his "gift" of insult and ignorance right back in his hands for him to keep. She calls him out with a next-level skillfulness, says (and without a shred of guilt), "No . . . *hell no!*" and broaches the difficult conversation without hesitation.

Shariputra, with his gender bias on full display, exposes that his cultural assumptions have gone unquestioned. He is, in fact, a victim of his own negativity bias and confirmation bias—that is, he assumed someone with characteristics other than his own to be inferior and, as evidence, he cited a societal norm with no basis in reality. It's the ancient Indian equivalent of reposting an article on social media without reading it or verifying its sources. As mentioned above, the presence of Prajnaparamita in the myth itself quietly asserts that her femaleness indeed matters, and yet she goes on to quote the Buddha: "In all things, there is neither male nor female." We can only conclude that her femaleness is intrinsic to her awakened state and yet that state itself is the product of her connection to an absolute beyond such characteristics. This exemplifies that Vedic mantra *achintya-bheda-abheda-tattva*, that all things are inconceivably and simultaneously diverse and yet part of the same supreme oneness—and that both of these distinctions are to be honored. Prajnaparamita's debate victory is a call-out enacted with skill and precision. It's also a moment that comes at the tail end of a long and hearty debate, when Prajnaparamita has engaged in much emotional labor and yet finds the resources to pull off her deepest act of the day.

The *Vimilakirti Sutra* reminds us that the need to confront oppression and dehumanization—systemically, interpersonally, and within our own hearts—is nothing new. Our spiritual intentions do not excuse us from having to do such work. In fact, quite the opposite—they align us with a tradition of living from vibrant love, a love that does not ignore the manifest, intersectional paradigm. I'm reminded of a recent picture of an older woman in a march holding up a sign that read "I can't believe I still have to protest this shit!" I thought of her as Prajnaparamita, two thousand years after the writing of the *Vimilakirti* mythos.

To live from vibrant love in a world where degrading structures prevail—this is both our predicament and its answer. The predicament: here we are, opening our hearts to compassion through meditation, working for an equitable world—or at least a world where torture, slavery, poverty, and public manipulation by the powerful are eradicated—and yet it is work that has no end. The answer: to live a life rooted in love for the world and all beings even if it is all unfixable. To care courageously in the middle of the tumult. To organize as an act of engaged meditation. To confront bigotry not because of our modern situation but because that is just what we do. To have compassion not because we expect it to be effective but because it is our ethos, our soul-imperative. To rise up unconditionally, for the sake of rising up. Even if we can't fix our world, how will we live? Even if no one is watching, what choices will we make? Even if our action bears no consequence, how will we act? Even if climate change were to decimate the planet tomorrow, let us go out protecting the planet and its inhabitants. Living for justice is not only about changing our social circumstances but also about being able to square up with our moral hearts when we face ourselves in the mirror at day's end.

The story of Prajnaparamita also confronts us with the paradox of expressing unity from a self that is fluid, multifaceted, simultaneously within and beyond our bodies, and that exceeds our definitions. If anyone "contains multitudes," it's her. And yet, at least in this story, she doesn't display her parts as disparate and conflicted. In this case it is Shariputra—an ardent practitioner of the Dharma, reputed to be possessed of his wisest parts—who allows the parts of him still abiding in ignorance to take over. To be the embodiment of transcendent wisdom, however, would be for one's inner system of parts to be acting together in well-coalesced harmony and confidence. That's the view of enlightenment in Buddhism: to be a loving and clear-seeing community unto oneself, within oneself, and then to impart this possibility in all outer, literal communities.

The Buddha foretold of a second coming, a "Buddha to be" who would reestablish sanity to a world in peril. The renowned Buddhist teacher and social activist Thich Nhat Hanh updated this prophecy by suggesting that this coming Buddha might not be a person at all but rather a *sangha*, a community. One can imagine a community so unified, so strong, and so wise that it alters the tide of destruction we are currently riding. Except, in this scenario, no one person holds all the strength, all the wisdom, all the love. Rather, respective members of the consortium hold individual aspects of it, and it is when they come together and collaborate that Awakened Love is made manifest. The prophesied Buddha, Buddha Maitreya, isn't about the feeling of love so much as about love in action, love as radical unity, structural love, systemic love. This is not a prophecy of salvation; it is a prophecy of our potential—a potential realized not by divine destiny but by intentional action. Help is not on the way. Help is already here. We are it. There is no other option. We must become the Buddha Maitreya. We must manifest our part. We must awaken love in the heat of the forest fires. We must attend to such work like our lives depend on it.

Because they do.

ACKNOWLEDGMENTS

With gratitude for their moral support and wise counsel, I acknowledge Louise Egger, Bonnie Pipkin, Adreanna Limbach, Lodro Rinzler, Amanda Gilbert, and Maxwell Wiggins.

With gratitude for each of their contributions, even if it did not end up being included, I acknowledge Leslie Booker, Nickie Tilsner, Nick Werber, Aaron Rose, and Shara Feldman.

With gratitude for opportunities for healing and growth, I acknowledge Richard Schwartz, Cristina Kartheiser, Reggie Ray, Neil McKinlay, Norman Elizondo, Jack Kornfield, Christina Tavera, Anne Roise and all at Spirit Rock, Shannon Iverson and all at Kripalu, the faculty at Omega Institute, my MNDFL family, my Maha Rose family, Sophia and Martin at Vertigo Rock Climbing, and Yancey Quezada and the team at The Grit Ninja.

With gratitude for coparenting this book into existence, I acknowledge Rachel Neumann, Matt Zepelin, KJ Grow, Breanna Locke, Katelin Ross, Ivan Bercholz, Sara Bercholz, and all at Shambhala Publications.

And to each of my teachers who appear in the form of clients and students, it is you to whom I owe most thanks of all. Where would I be without you?

NOTES

1. Jason Silverstein, "There Have Been More Mass Shootings Than Days This Year," *CBS News*, November 15, 2019, www.cbsnews.com/news/mass-shootings-2019-more-massshootings-than-days-so-far-this-year.
2. I borrow the concept of "unblending" from the IFS model. See Richard C. Schwartz and Martha Sweezy, *Internal Family Systems Therapy, Second Edition* (New York: Guilford Press, 2019), 43.
3. Gil Press, "6 Predictions for the $203 Billion Big Data Analytics Market," *Forbes*, January 20, 2017, www.forbes.com/sites/gilpress/2017/01/20/6-predictions-for-the-203-billion-big-data-analytics-market/#675f79202083.
4. Marshall Rosenberg, "Memnoon Concept," YouTube video, 1:32, www.youtube.com/watch?v=lMJE7cR_I2Y.
5. Christine Vendel, "'She Didn't Know What Was Real': Did 10-Day Meditation Retreat Trigger Woman's Suicide?" *Penn Live*, January 5, 2019, www.pennlive.com/news/2017/06/york_county_suicide_megan_vogt.html.
6. For more on trauma and mindfulness meditation, see David A. Treleavan, *Trauma-Sensitive Mindfulness: Practices for Safe and Transformative Healing* (New York: W. W. Norton, 2018).

7. Danny Givertz, "Play Therapy . . . It's Not Just for Kids," Well Clinic, July 10, 2019, www.wellsanfrancisco.com /play-therapy-for-adults.

8. Andrea Zaccaro et al., "How Breath-Control Can Change Your Life: A Systematic Review on Psycho-Physiological Correlates of Slow Breathing," *Frontiers in Human Neuroscience* 12, September 7, 2018, www.ncbi.nlm.nih.gov /pmc/articles/PMC6137615.

9. World Hunger Education Service, "2018 World Hunger and Poverty Facts and Statistics," Hunger Notes, www .worldhunger.org/world-hunger-and-poverty-facts-and-statistics.

10. Elisabeth Rosenthal and Andrew Martin, "UN Says Solving Food Crisis Could Cost $30 Billion," *New York Times*, June 4, 2008, www.nytimes.com/2008/06/04 /news/04iht-04food.13446176.html.

11. Jeremy Erdman, "We Produce Enough Food to Feed 10 Billion People. So Why Does Hunger Still Exist?" *Medium*, February 1, 2018, https://medium.com/@jeremyerdman/we-produce-enough-food-to-feed-10-billion -people-so-why-does-hunger-still-exist-8086d2657539.

12. "World Population Day: July 11, 2018," United States Census Bureau, August 1, 2018, www.census.gov/newsroom/stories/2018/world-population.html.

ABOUT THE AUTHOR

Ralph De La Rosa, LCSW, is a psychotherapist in private practice and a seasoned meditation instructor. He began practicing meditation in 1996 and has taught since 2008. He was a student of Amma's (Mata Amritanandamayi) for sixteen years and began studying Buddhism in 2005. His work has been featured in the *New York Post, CNN, GQ, Self, Women's Health,* and many other publications and podcasts. He regularly leads immersive healing retreats at Omega Institute, Spirit Rock, and Kripalu. He is a summa cum laude graduate of Fordham University's social work program and has trained in multiple forms of trauma-focused treatment, including Internal Family Systems therapy and Somatic Experiencing.

Ralph himself is a depression, PTSD, and opiate addiction survivor. His work is inspired by the tremendous transformation he has experienced through meditation, yoga, and therapy.